`T0160191`

# ADVANCE PRAISE

"What a unique pleasure it is to watch David do his thing. His energy, enthusiasm and true passion for helping people comes through immediately."

—SCOTT MILRAD
*Content Manager, Business, LinkedIn Corporation*

"Rockstar Customer Service is a proven, real-world system on how to provide excellent customer service, and nobody does it better than David."

—FORBES RILEY
*CEO/ Founder, SpinGym and Celebrity TV Host*

"David's customer service content is superb and will help you and your organization get the results you are after."

—JASON BROOK
*Founder, Healthy Commerce Inc.*

"Rockstar Customer Service helped our company tremendously by taking our customer service to world-class status with our Fortune 500 clients. Without Rockstar Customer Service, we not be at the level we are at today."

—RICKY ARRIOLA
*CEO, Inktel Contact Center Solutions*

"We had a lull in our customer service. The strategies of Rockstar Customer Service helped us grow 30 percent year over year."

—MATHEW FINK
*CEO, Comfort Keepers Home Care*

"Before Rockstar Customer Service, we were struggling with giving our customers great service. After Rockstar Customer Service, client retention went up and our team goes above and beyond for our customers."

—ADAM FLORES
*CEO, Business Club Academy*

# ROCKSTAR SERVICE, ROCKSTAR PROFITS

# ROCKSTAR
## *Service*
# ROCKSTAR
## *Profits*

### Increase Your Revenues,
### Grow Your Business and
### Create Raving Fan Customers for Life

# DAVID BROWNLEE

NEW YORK

LONDON • NASHVILLE • MELBOURNE • VANCOUVER

# ROCKSTAR SERVICE, ROCKSTAR PROFITS

*Increase Your Revenues, Grow Your Business and Create Raving Fan Customers for Life*

Published in New York, New York, by Morgan James Publishing. Morgan James is a trademark of Morgan James, LLC. www.MorganJamesPublishing.com

ISBN 9781642792225 paperback
ISBN 9781642792232 eBook
Library of Congress Control Number: 2018954172

**Cover & Interior Design by:**
Christopher Kirk
www.GFSstudio.com

Morgan James is a proud partner of Habitat for Humanity Peninsula and Greater Williamsburg. Partners in building since 2006.

Get involved today! Visit
MorganJamesPublishing.com/giving-back

*To my parents. Thank you for always believing in me, encouraging me and loving me.*

*To my sister, Crystal. You are always there for me to lift me up and make me smile. Thank you.*

*To my fans, followers, and clients. Thank you for the opportunity to serve you and live my passion every day.*

*To my children, Angelo and Sofia. You are amazing human beings and daddy loves you very much.*

*To my wife, Luna. Thank you for sticking by me through thick and thin, and supporting me emotionally and spiritually through this journey. I love you.*

# TABLE OF CONTENTS

# ACKNOWLEDGEMENTS

Thank you to my rockstar team for a job well done in taking this book from my head to reality. Tony Robbins, Brendon Burchard, Forbes Riley, Jason Brook, Marc Von Musser, Eric Brown, David Hancock, Jim Howard, Bonnie Rauch, Sharon Kaplan, Ricky Arriola, Scott Milrad, Adam Flores, Mathew Fink and all of my fans from around the world. I care about each and every one of you and could not have done this without you. Thank you for you inspiring me when I didn't feel inspired and getting me through this process with your unwavering support.

# FOREWORD

February 15, 2008, was a day that changed David Brownlee's life forever. After surviving being kidnapped at gunpoint and stabbed, he decided to dedicate his life to helping others. He founded The Pure Customer Service Training Company and became an international speaker, trainer, and coach sharing his story and inspiring audiences all over the world.

After a career in the corporate world, he became a serial entrepreneur obsessed with serving customers at the highest level. David sold a successful entertainment and events company after growing the business for 10 years. His mission is to help 100 million businesses and individuals find success through kindness and respect for others. David believes it all starts in our businesses and that as business owners, entrepreneurs, managers, and employees, we are the ones who will change the world for the better.

A successful entrepreneur for more than 20 years, and former business coach and seminar leader for Tony Robbins,

David has conducted over 3,500 one-on-one coaching sessions and trained over 1 million organizations and individuals globally. He has put together a world-class team of coaches, facilitators, and support staff to deliver lasting results to clients faster, easier, and with better results.

David's goal with this book is to create a ripple effect of people treating each other better. His hope is that the readers of this book will go back to their offices and treat their employees better. Then those employees will go home and treat their families better. David believes that you have the power to create a positive, never-ending ripple effect that will reverberate throughout the world. The world could use a little more kindness and caring toward one another, couldn't it?

Thank you for embarking on this journey with David to help create something positive for all of us.

—SEAN KIRSCHENSTEIN

*CEO, Founder, Languagefish LLC*

# PREFACE

I am David Brownlee, founder of The Pure Customer Service Training Company and creator of The Pure Customer Service Certification Program. Before we start, I just want to say thank you for choosing my book, *Rockstar Service, Rockstar Profits*, to improve your customer service skills and knowledge—whether it's to increase your customer database, improve your online reviews, increase your revenues and grow your business, or even to get that promotion or pay raise in your customer service job.

Whatever your reason, I commend you for taking the time to read this book to better your skills and to continue learning. I hope that you get great value from it.

Customer service is my passion! I'm lucky to be able to train people on this subject every day. I absolutely love it. Throughout my career, I've worked in several businesses, from large Fortune 500 companies to restaurants and small businesses. The one thing that I found in any successful business, big or small, is that customer service is the key to a company's success. Specifically, Rockstar Customer Service is the key to a company's success.

What do I mean by that? Imagine for a moment that you are going about your daily business as usual when you get a phone call. Mick Jagger (or Paul McCartney—Stones versus Beatles) is interested in your company. They need your product or service. Or better yet, they actually come in to your place of business and need your help. After you "come to" from fainting and wipe the drool off your mouth (fellas, this exercise works with Beyoncé or fill in the blank), what would you say to them? How would you treat them? What lengths would you go to in order to make sure they are well taken care of? How would you entice them to tell their famous friends about you and your company? What would you offer them to come back? I'm guessing the service you strive to provide them would be pretty stellar.

The idea of doing business with rockstars can be an exciting thought. To me, an even more exciting thought is treating your customers that come in to your business every day like rockstars. They will tell all of their friends (famous or not) how great you and your business are. They will come back to your business over and over again. They will write great things about you online for the world to see resulting in raving fan clients that are excited to do business with you.

You may be thinking, "But David, I run a small business, and I don't have the tools, time, or money to implement a customer service program like the big companies to create raving fan customers." Here's the good news. You don't have to. Creating raving fan clients is easier than ever to do. It's not expensive either. In this book, you'll learn how to gain client referrals, get more positive online reviews, increase your sales and grow your business. Without customers, your business can't exist, right? At least, not for very long.

Over the years, I've started and sold numerous businesses in different industries and have always done my best to implement the strategies I've learned and the tools I've discovered in customer service. These are the same concepts that you will be learning throughout this book. I've had the pleasure of training over a million businesses and individuals in customer service, and I'm excited to continue doing so with you.

This book will help you increase your revenues, build a loyal customer base, increase your customer referrals, and get you more positive online reviews. And if you're a customer service representative, it will definitely help you to be better, more confident, and more successful in your job—and enhance your career.

Thanks for reading, and enjoy!

*"A customer is the most important visitor on our premises. He is not dependent on us. We are dependent on him. He is not an interruption in our work. He is the purpose of it. He is not an outsider in our business. He is a part of it. We are not doing him a favor by serving him. He is doing us a favor by giving us an opportunity to do so."*

—MAHATMA GANDHI

*"People expect good service but few are willing to give it."*

—ROBERT GATELY, AUTHOR

# INTRODUCTION

If you're reading this, congratulations! You have made the decision to take your customer service to the next level. The next chapters and pages could be the most important you'll read to boost the success of your company's customer service strategy. You'll be focusing and working *on* your customer service instead of *in* your customer service. And the reason this is so important is because as executives, managers, and customer service professionals, we rarely have the time or the energy to plan, innovate, and implement new customer service strategies. When we do finally take the time, it helps us grow our client base exponentially, improve communication with our internal clients, build a loyal and vocal fan base of clients, and increase referrals and revenues that will have a huge impact on your paycheck.

Some of your peers may say you're *crazy* for investing in a customer service book. But what could be more noble and impactful than improving your relationship with your clients and providing them with a world-class experience? That should be commended.

What if there was a way to use customer service strategies to double your revenues this year? What if you could learn to enjoy coming to work each day and engage with your co-workers and customers in a way that would boost their interest in your company? Would you like to double the number of referrals you get in 30 days or less? Does all of this sound crazy? I'm here to tell you it's not. I have had the privilege of training more than a million businesses and individuals from around the world to do just that. I have been teaching successful customer service through my online training, live events, and coaching programs. I have clients who have doubled their revenues in six months and doubled their number of referrals just by using the techniques you're about to learn. By delivering your customers a world-class experience, you will increase your profits and make more money.

I understand the importance of time, because once it's gone, you can't get it back. That's why I promise this book will clearly show you the best practices, proven strategies, and shortcuts from my years of expertise to help you close the gap between where you are today in customer service and where you want to be. After 20 years as an entrepreneur and a customer service fanatic, and after conducting thousands of one-on-one coaching calls, thousands of hours of research, and countless case studies, I've done all the work. I've discovered the patterns that lead to success in customer service as well as the patterns that lead to failure. In this book, you will discover the strategies, the blueprints, and the concepts used by me and some of the most successful companies in the world.

This book is for business owners and executives, managers and supervisors, customer service representatives, and employees who come in contact with customers or co-workers. As you read through the concepts and strategies, apply them specifically to your position, and imagine how they can help you take your customer service skills to the next level.

This book is designed to help you achieve your goals in customer service and customer loyalty. I wrote this book with the beginner in mind, the intermediate customer service employee in mind, and the advanced customer service organizations and individuals in mind. So, for example, if you recently started working in a customer service position or you were recently promoted to your company's customer service department, or you have started a new business—or maybe you've never had any customer service training until now—this book is for you. If you or your organization are at an intermediate level, you can absolutely skip around to the chapters that will help you gain more insight into specific questions you have about boosting your customer service or the number of referrals you want get, etc. If you are a company known for its world-class customer service but are looking for ways to continue to grow and implement new cutting-edge strategies, feel free to visit the chapters that will guide you along that path.

Wherever you are starting from or however you got here, I'm glad to be here with you. I'm honored to be your personal customer service coach, and I'm excited for the opportunity to help you grow your revenues and boost your paychecks with these tips and lessons.

Let's get down to some specifics.

You might be asking yourself, "What am I going to take away from your book?" First, you are going to discover your world-class customer service roadmap. My book will help you assess where you are now and where you want to go.

Next, you will learn why customer service is important and how you get leverage for yourself and your company to make change possible. You will learn about a technique called "minding your brain." You will learn about the psychology of customer service and how it affects you and your customers in your company culture.

You also will learn how to truly understand what your customers want from you and how to deliver world-class service to them, how to respond to a customer's needs, and the responsibility that comes with it. This includes learning about the importance of empathy and how to use it in customer service.

After that, you will learn about clarification, which will save you time, money, and energy.

This book will give you the tools to discover how to earn the privilege of a customer's referrals as well as their loyalty to your product or service. You will learn how to turn those customers and clients into what I call "raving fan clients" who will never leave you. After you've turned the final page in this book, it's my hope that you'll walk away with more than just having learned *why* you need to deliver excellent customer service but also *how* to do it consistently. What this book will do is provide you with a very clear blueprint, strategy, and tactical plan of action for implementing what you've learned. I will not tell you how to run your business. You are the expert in your industry and in running your company. My tools will only add to the skills you already possess.

My passion and expertise is in customer service, and my mission is to help you find fulfillment in life and business through kindness and service so that you can deliver that through your customer experience. The program I developed changed my business and my life. In fact, it literally saved my life. And now I am passing it on by assisting clients through online programs, certifications, live events, and coaching.

My journey over the last two decades, in business and in life, has been amazing. Chock full of lessons, learning, and growth. In the next few pages I'll share with you the stories that have brought me here with you today.

But first, I want to share with you what makes this approach to customer service training different from what you have experienced before. For the past several years, I have been a high-performance business coach. I was lucky to have one of the most successful mentors in this space, Tony Robbins. When I joined his business results coaching team, I knew I was in the right place to serve clients. In a relatively short span, I conducted over 2,500 one-on-one coaching sessions. I obsessed over how the brain works and how it affects our productivity at work. Finding out why we do or do not take certain actions helped me accelerate success with my clients. I can quickly recognize the patterns in clients that are holding them back from their success or propelling them forward. I have incorporated what I have discovered into this book. That way, you are getting world-class customer service strategies and the psychological insight and tools that will help inject lasting change into your organization. My hope is that you achieve your desired outcomes faster, easier, and with better results. As the CEO of PureCustomerService. com, it is my responsibility to make sure we accomplish our mission: "To help 100 million businesses and individuals find success in customer service through kindness, respect, and caring for one another in our businesses." Our world could use a little more kindness, respect, and caring for one another, couldn't it?

We accomplish this through our books, online customer service training programs, live seminars, and coaching programs. We are grateful every day for the opportunity to serve you and help transform your business through rockstar customer service strategies.

✷ ✷ ✷

So, who is this David Brownlee guy? Let me give you a quick snapshot of how I came to be with you today. I live in San Diego with my wife and two young kids. This is the greatest time of my life. But it wasn't always great.

Back in the day, I was young man living in Los Angeles, playing in a band, and dabbling in acting. I would constantly ask myself, "Will I be the next Denzel Washington or the next rockstar or both?" But reality set in pretty quickly: The acting gigs started dying out, the record deal fell through, and I was left wondering what I was going to do.

Luckily, I have degree in speech communications, so I headed straight for the corporate world. One of my favorite jobs was helping launch a natural juice brand here on the West Coast. I started selling the juice on a street corner here in Southern California to a small café and continued to watch the brand grow throughout my territory. Everything was going great. It wasn't long before another little company—OK, it was a big company—came to the founders with a dump truck full of money. They sold the company to the bigger fish. No more juice for me.

At the time, I was in a relationship that ended badly. So, I didn't know what I was going to do with my career or with my life. Whatever you do, never ask yourself if things can get worse. They really can. I had spent all of my money and ended up living on my best friend's dining room floor on a mattress. One day, he had the good sense to sit me down and say, "Look, David, if you can help build a company for someone else, maybe you can build up *your own* company." Great advice! (Though I'm sure he wanted his dining room back, too.) And that's exactly what I did. I started my first company from that mattress in that dining room.

I had some experience as a DJ, so I started a DJ company, which I expanded to include lighting and video production, and before I knew it, I was running a full blown special-events company. I went from living on that mattress to buying my own house and earning six figures within 12 months. I was driven! And it all started with a decision: I wouldn't live another day nor another second in a terrible situation. We've all gone through some kind of adversity in our lives. Change starts with a decision; maybe it was the decision to buy this book to take your customer service to the next level.

When I first started this production and entertainment company, I didn't know where I was going to find clients. I was lucky to be in Los Angeles because a lot of the clients I wanted to work with were in the entertainment industry. But it's a very tight-knit industry, and referrals are currency, and I didn't know how to get them. I had zero referrals. So, I started researching how to get referrals and how to build a customer experience that makes my clients so happy and thrilled that they start telling their friends about my business. My research paid off. I went from zero referrals to having a business that was over 90 percent referrals. When I finally cracked the code, it totally transformed my company. I expanded very quickly. But this growth also cost me a lot of time, money, and resources—and endless frustration.

The next part of this story is where things get serious. A 45-minute encounter that would change my life forever and deliver me front and center to over half a million businesses and individuals from around the globe and counting. A 45-minute encounter that was a matter of life or death.

My business started to grow—and with that growth came a lot of pressure. I needed to relax. I would often go to Central America for vacations. During one of my trips there, I visited a friend of mine who lived there. I had always found myself envious of his lifestyle. He said, "David, you know what? You can have all this, too—the white sand beaches, palm trees, relaxation." He was right! My business, at the time, was practically running itself, so I said, "You know what, I'm going to do it. I'm going to take a mid-life sabbatical." Before I left Los Angeles, I met the woman who would become my wife, and she agreed to go with me. We shared this wonderful experience together. I learned my three S's: surf, salsa, and Spanish.

It was an absolutely magical experience until one fateful night in February 2008. My wife and I were going to meet some friends in Managua—the country's biggest city—where a brand-new sushi restaurant had opened up. We were excited and decided to make a weekend out of it. As we were getting ready to leave for the restaurant, I was thinking to myself, "We should take a cab. Maybe I'll even enjoy a sake."

The hotel ordered a cab for us, and we went out to dinner and had a great meal. As we were getting ready to leave the restaurant, instead of asking the hostess to call us a cab, I spotted one dropping off a fare. I said, "Babe, there's a cab right there. Let's go grab it." We got in, and the cabdriver began the trip home.

After a few minutes, the driver pulled the car over to the side of the road. There wasn't a lot of activity in this part of town, just some empty fields. He said, "Tengo que urinar," (I have to urinate). My wife and I thought that was weird—but the guy's got to do what he got to do. He came back a few minutes later, and we started driving again. We had the windows down and music playing—"Eye of the Tiger" was on the radio, and we were jamming along to it—and then he pulled over again. This time, the front passenger door opened up, and somebody got in. Again, we thought it was strange, but Nicaragua has a rideshare system called, a cooperativo, similar to Uber Pool—where you share a ride with somebody and then split the fare at the end. So, not totally weird ... but it was about to be.

When we were within five minutes of the hotel, he pulled over *again*. This time, somebody else got in the backseat—with my wife and me.

So, imagine this: You've got the cabdriver in the driver's seat, somebody in the front passenger seat, me behind the cabdriver, my wife in the middle next to me, and now this other man sitting next to my wife. The door closed … and we got that sinking feeling that something was wrong.

Before I knew it, the guy in the front passenger seat was pointing a gun in my face and yelling, "La plata, plata (Give me your money)!" My instincts kicked in. You don't know how you're going to react until you're in a situation like that. I grabbed the gunman by the wrists in a way that he couldn't shoot me and in that same second, the guy sitting next to my wife, who turned out to be his partner, pulled out a knife. He saw me wrestling with the gun and tried to stab me in my midsection. I scooted out of the way, but he managed to cut me and pull the knife back. Before I knew it, he drew the knife again and plunged it deep into my thigh and pulled the knife back out. Blood was spurting everywhere. At that moment, I knew I had to take control of the situation.

I knew I had to go from conflict to something involving caring and kindness, from violence to calm. So, what did I do? I started talking. I talked him down and started focusing on what it was these men really wanted. They wanted my money. So, I got them to take us to a bank. We pulled out as much as we could from the ATM. After they got the money, they wanted our cell phones—and they wanted my wife's wedding ring.

Several years before this incident in the cab, my dad passed away. He had always wanted to go to Italy, but before we got the chance to go with him, cancer had taken him from us.

I actually proposed to my wife in Italy, in Venice, on a gondola. It was amazing. I asked the gondolier to take us somewhere private because I was going to ask her to marry me. He says, "Oh, *signor*. Don't worry I've got the perfect place!" He took us through the canals in Venice, the air was crisp, and I took out the ring and asked her to marry me. She said yes, and next thing I knew, there was clapping and cheering. We had drifted under a bridge of people who were smiling at us and applauding.

My wife is from Italy, and she wanted me to see the Bridge of Sighs. After I proposed, she said, "We can go to the Bridge of Sighs, and we can think about your dad and connect with him." I thought it was a beautiful idea. We went to dinner first, and, as we're eating, I hear my dad's favorite song, "The Shadow of Your Smile," wafting in from outside. A guitar player happened to be sitting on the corner near the restaurant playing this particularly sentimental song. We walked out of the restaurant, went over to the musician, and gave him a tip. I asked him if could tell us where the Bridge of Sighs is. He replied, "You're standing on it." He was playing my dad's favorite song on the Bridge of Sighs where were already planning to go to honor his memory. What a moment! I had just proposed, and her ring became this magical piece that bonded both of us together.

The men in the cab were trying to get everything they could from us, but my wife took off her wedding ring when they weren't looking and sat on it so they couldn't see it. They had all the other things, but they didn't get that ring. When we look back on that incident and talk about it, we talk about how that ring was our protector that stayed with us.

We drove around in that cab for another 45 minutes. They made a right turn, and drove us up a hill toward an area that could best be described as the Beverly Hills of Managua. There are huge, beautiful estates with gates and guards. I said, "Oh, this is looking good." My elation quickly disappeared. The car kept driving up a winding road that led to another road that led to a pitch-black field. The cab turned and started slowly driving down a gravel road. The lights from the big houses behind us were getting dimmer and dimmer and dimmer.

The car stopped, the door opened, and one of the men said, "Get out! Get on your knees!" We did. Then one of the men said, "Close your eyes!" We closed our eyes. As my wife and I waited there, waiting for the next horrible sound, we heard the taxi driving away.

We were alive.

I was still bleeding like a stuck pig from a stab wound to my leg, but we stood up and began walking toward the estates we passed during the ordeal. It was like a scene from a really bad horror movie, where the characters are walking back to safety as the credits start rolling. Finally, we made it to one of the big houses. It had a guard out in front, and we told him what happened. He went in and called the owners, and they called an ambulance. Eventually, we wrote a letter to the embassy and told them what happened.

You know how people say when you experience a near-death experience your whole life flashes before your eyes? That's not what happened to me.

I asked myself questions. For me, those questions were really simple: Did I make a difference? Was I kind and caring to the people around me, and did I experience true love? Those are life's most important questions. It didn't matter how big my house was or what kind of car I owned or even how successful my businesses were. The answers to those very simple questions showed me what was really important and that I had a second chance to do something positive with my life. I believe that's why I survived that experience. I decided that meant living my life to help others. I thought about all the people I coached and mentored, and I said, "This is it!" This is what my life was going to be all about: helping people transform their lives or their businesses every single day. And that's how I ended up where I am today. It is my goal—my mission in life—to guide you so that you can experience success in your life—whatever that means to you. And if I can be the catalyst to help get you there, then that's my mission. I am honored to be on this journey with you.

And with all this in mind, we are going to dive right in!

*"I've learned that people will forget what you said, people will forget what you did, but people will never forget how you made them feel."*

—MAYA ANGELOU

*"Kind words can be short and easy to speak, but their echoes are truly endless."*

—MOTHER TERESA

# ⭐ 1

# GET HONEST

> One-third of customers say they would
> "rather clean a toilet" than speak with a
> customer service representative.

magine for a moment that you are going about your day, business as usual when you get a phone call. Mick Jagger (or Paul McCartney—Stones versus Beatles) is interested in your company. Or imagine *YOUR* favorite musician, actor or celebrity. They need your product or service. Or better yet, they actually come in to your place of business and need your help that you can provide them. After you come to from fainting and wipe the drool off your mouth (fellas, this exercise works with Beyoncé or fill in the blank), What would you say to them? How would you treat them? What length would you go to and make sure they are well taken care of? How would you entice them to tell their famous friends about you and your company?

What would you offer them to come back? No ask yourself this question, "When was the last time you or your staff treated your customers in this way?"

The idea of doing business with rockstars can be an exciting thought. To me, an even more exciting thought is treating your customers that actually come into your business every day like rockstars. They will tell all of their friends (famous or not) how great you and your business are. They will come back to your business over and over again. They will write great things about you online for the world to see. Resulting in raving fan clients that are excited to do business with you again and again. Keep this attitude in mind—treating every client or customer like you would your favorite rockstar as you read through this book.

You may be thinking, "But David, I am a small business, and I don't have the tools, time or money to implement a customer service program like the big companies to create raving fan customers." Here's the good news. You don't have to. Creating raving fan clients is easier than ever to do. It's not expensive either. In this book, you'll learn how to gain client referrals, get more positive online reviews, increase your sales and grow your business.

In this chapter, we are going to talk about Secret No. 1: You have to be honest!

But what does it really mean to be honest with yourself and honest about your company? In order to improve your customer service, you have to be honest about where you are *today*. By starting right here and right now, we can put together a map to get you from where you are to where you want to be.

I have worked with tons of companies that put on a façade. On the outside, they're telling customers, "Hey, we are great with our customers!" But when you get there, the experience is a disaster! I do a lot of what's called "mystery shopping." Basically, I call up a company's customer service line or go to the store itself as though I am a real customer—and I get to experience firsthand what the customers are experiencing. A lot of times, it's not as awesome as the company implies. It's just horrible. If you are someone who's identified that there is something wrong internally with your company, it's OK to be honest with yourself and honest with your company about where you really are.

Next, I want to talk about the meaning of the term "world class." What does world class mean to you? Before we dive into that, can you answer a question: Who won the 100-meter dash during the Brazil Olympics in 2016? Do you remember? It was Usain Bolt of Jamaica. He ran 100 meters in 9.81 seconds. He is the fastest man alive. So, is Usain Bolt world class? I would say yes. Whether you're a sports fan or not, that guy is quantifiably the best of the best. In fact, when he trains, he works so hard that he pukes afterwards—and he's only practicing. He gets up to that starting mark with his coach, gets on the track, and runs his heart out, pushing himself harder and harder. When was the last time you pushed yourself so hard during customer service training that you puked? *Kidding!* But you get my point. Pushing yourself beyond what everybody else is doing is the first step toward being world class at what you do.

Now that you know Usain Bolt won the 100-meter dash in 9.81 seconds, do you know who came in second? It was Justin Gatlin, an American who ran it in 9.89 seconds. Who came in third place? That was Andre De Grasse from Canada; he ran it in 9.91 seconds. What about fourth place? I recently asked a class if anyone knew who came in fourth place, and a guy answered, "Who cares? It doesn't matter!" It's kind of funny, but he is the fourth fastest person in the world. Well, it was Yohan Blake, and he ran it in 9.93 seconds. All four of these runners were separated by less than a second as far as speed goes. You just read about the top four fastest guys *in the world*, but many of you probably didn't know who won fourth place.

So, where are you in your marketplace? Are you Usain Bolt? Are you No. 1? Are you world-class? Before you answer, I personally believe that No. 4 is still passing in terms of good customer service—but is that how your clients would see you? That's a big question. If you can't remember the names of the second, third, or fourth fastest man in the world—if you can only remember who is No. 1—that should tell you something about being world class.

I'll give you another example. There is a hotel where my wife and I spent our anniversary. We wanted to do something really special. We decided to drive up the coast and get a hotel right on the water with a beautiful view. The hotel chain we chose is known for its service. It builds its brand based on that service. As soon as we pulled up, the valet—his name was Parker—was so happy to see us. He was genuinely excited. He got out and shook our hands.

He said, "Hey, Welcome! What's your name?"

"Mr. Brownlee."

"Mr. Brownlee, we've been expecting you!"

"You have?"

I mean I hadn't even gotten out of my car yet. When we finally did and went to the back, there was already a bellman gathering our luggage out of the trunk. He took all of it and walked us right up to the counter to check in. The concierge said, "Mr. Brownlee, we've been expecting you! Happy anniversary!" He knew it was our anniversary. I had told another man earlier, but now this gentleman brought it up, too. He made me feel like a rockstar.

As my wife and I walked with the bellman to our room, he made polite conversation and told us about the hotel and asked us what we would like to do. He engaged with us and helped us make our stay even more fantastic. When we got up to the room—which was gorgeous—what do you think was waiting for us? Flowers, chocolates, and a little card that said, "Happy anniversary." That's world class! And that's the lesson: What is your business doing to be world class like that?

This is a big hotel chain, and you may be thinking, "But I'm a small business! I can't afford to give flowers and chocolates to all of our clients." Maybe not. But it's not the flowers or the chocolates that make them world class. It is how the staff made me feel as a customer, as a client! Later on in this book, I will be teaching you a little bit about the psychology of your customers.

If we're going to take you from where you are to where you want to be, we need to be honest. So, where are you right now? Let's use a metaphor. I like metaphors. We're going to take a road trip from L.A. to New York. We are going to drive. We need to know where our starting point is because we're going to enter it into our GPS. We need to know our destination.

Let's imagine our favorite rockstar is playing a concert in New York on a specific date and time. We *really* want to go to that concert. If we like that band enough, we're going to do *whatever it takes* to see them perform. That's the kind of road-map you are going to set for your customer service goals. You are going to know exactly where you're starting from, exactly where you're going, and exactly what it's going to take to get there. If you don't know where you are starting from, you'll never get to where you want to go. That's true for customer service, and it's true in life.

> # 84% of customers say that their last customer service interaction did not exceed their expectations.

This part of chapter 1 is going to take a deep dive into the history of customer service—old school versus new school. We're going to look at the customer service timeline.

We'll pick four different places in time: the 1950s, 1990s, mid-2000s, and 2020. Did you ever see *Back to the Future* with Michael J. Fox? It was a great movie. There is a particular scene after Fox's character arrives back in time to the '50s to his hometown. He's disoriented, and he looks around and spots a gas station. A car pulls into the gas station, a little bell goes "ding, ding," and four attendants come running out wearing hats and bowties while the song "Mr. Sandman" plays in the background. Do you remember that scene? They come running out, and one guy is wiping the windshield, one is pumping the gas, another guy is checking the oil, and a fourth guy is pumping air into the tires. When was the last time you had that experience at a gas station? What happened to that level of customer service?

Back in the '50s, small towns created a real sense of community. Everybody knew each other, and businesses knew that the members of their community were their livelihood. If you owned a hardware store, you had a keen sense of customer appreciation. You understood that Mr. and Mrs. Smith were putting food on *your* table. These small businesses really made their customers feel welcome and special. The most important part of doing that was creating relationships—real relationships! Having a real relationship with somebody creates a loyal customer. In this section, we're going to discuss how that applies today in the 21st century.

Let's talk about the 1990s—because this is when customer service really began to change. The world was going through a tech boom. Companies were creating unique products for customers with home computers. Remember when MapQuest came out? I do—because it blew my mind! I couldn't believe I could just log in and look at my house from a satellite ... on my computer! I mean, it was via a dial-up modem, and it took a while to render, but there it was. We had a lot of innovative products like this back in the '90s, and their popularity grew exponentially. Tech companies realized that the world wanted and needed their products, so they started charging an arm and a leg for them—and the bottom line was born.

Companies began operating with the attitude of entitlement—"If you want my product, you've got to come to me." The customer was no longer special. It was all about the product and the stock market (which, at that time, was going through the roof), and the shareholders. These things were always important, but in the 1990s, companies shifted away from the consumer.

It's no surprise, then, that in the '90s the world was introduced to voice prompts. The companies no longer felt they needed people to talk to customers or clients. Instead, they sent customers through an endless maze of voice-prompted options for customer service. Pushing 0 would *sometimes* get you a human operator. That didn't last long. What happens now when you press 0 for an operator? "Sorry, we don't recognize that request." Click. Is that the experience you want your customer to have?

When you get on the phone with a customer service representative today, and you want to ask a quick question, their response is usually: "You know you can get your question answered on our website. Stop calling us!" They don't literally say that … but that's definitely the sentiment.

Let's review: Starting in the '50s, you have a special relationship with your clients; you are taking care of them and treating them like they're special. In the '90s, we see the advent of voice prompts and the outsourcing of customer service to people in other countries who have a completely different culture. Some representatives may not even speak English well enough to communicate with you or empathize with you, or really understand your problem. It's no fault of theirs; this was a corporate-level decision for dealing with customers.

Now, let's look ahead to the mid-2000s. We have technology like social media and online review sites (which we'll talk about in more detail later). In the 21st century, your customer now has a voice whether you like it or not. There are now online review sites where your prospective customers can read about what's happening with your business. Your customers can now see—almost in real time—how you are treating them and what kind of experience others are having with your business. This is a game-changer.

Research shows that, by 2020, 89 percent of businesses will be competing for customers and customer service. For example, someone will come up with a successful business concept or product, and what happens the very next month? A million other nearly identical versions pop up. More choices. Some products might be better or worse—and they will be offered at different price points with more features to choose from. As technology gets better, it will be easier to duplicate and improve upon different ideas. Studies also show that 85 percent of transactions will be made without human contact—85 percent! We're moving toward an era in which customer service still exists but without humans to do it. Technology is important to consider if you are a customer service representative: What does it mean for your job if your company replaces you with a robot?

What will distinguish a business among the fray? If you are a business owner who doesn't have any humans talking to customers, what are your customer service rules and procedures? What is the actual mindset that you are going to put into your customer service plan for treating your customers well? The opportunity for customer service representatives now is to step up their game and start showing the value their humanity brings to a company's bottom line and reputation—and getting clients to spread the word about how great their company is. That's the future. And it is not too far off. We need to start thinking now about what we're going to do in the future.

The old-school 1950s methods saw businesses developing great relationships and a community. During the '90s, businesses veered away from that mindset and created big corporations, big-box stores, and no relationships—zero. This, in turn, increased customer frustration. In the mid-2000s, it's shifting back to customers having a voice, and companies need to pay attention. If you want your company to be around in the future, you are going to need to create customer service core values and mission statements. You are going to need to have procedures that align with what the customers actually need and want. Frustrating your clients is not going to keep you in business. Make sense? Awesome!

Each year, businesses lose $41 billion due to poor customer service.

Now we're going to talk about the challenges that you might be facing in customer service today. We've all experienced these frustrations—as representatives and customers. Why is customer service so frustrating today? What happens when you are not delivering world-class customer service?

Here's a story you might be able to relate to. Recently, I bought a laptop computer. Instead of going to the store of the company that manufactures the computer, I went to one of the big-box stores. A computer I bought died not long after I got it, and I needed to get another one ASAP. I didn't have time to wait for shipping, so I went to this big-box company. After a long wait at the store, I finally found somebody to help me. I told the employee I wanted to buy a new computer—so a purchase of a couple thousand dollar—but he didn't seem super enthusiastic about selling me one. He was half-heartedly showing me different models, and I was asking him questions about them when suddenly this lady came up and interrupted our conversion. She says, "I'm trying to find pens." The guy literally turned to her and said, "OK! Yeah, let's go" and took off. I never saw the guy again. I couldn't believe it. Here I am trying to give the store my money—thousands of dollars—and the guy just leaves me to go help the lady looking for pens.

You get where I'm going with this, right? I went to the manager and had a conversation, and I said, "That's kind of unprofessional." He responds by telling me, "Yeah. They don't make a lot of commission on these so they are not very happy to help you." I looked at him and said, "Are you kidding me?" He said, "No. It happens." That was it. That was the manager's response.

Are you experiencing these challenges when it comes to providing world-class customer service for your company? Are your staff members rude to your clients? Are you or your team members having difficulty overcoming customer complaints? The key is to be prepared and know exactly how you are going to overcome customer rejection.

Ask yourselves: Are you or your employees committed to providing excellent customer service? What do I mean by that? Most of us think we know customer service. On the surface, customer service reps know that, at minimum, they need to *provide* excellent customer service. But are they really *committed* to it? A lot of companies maintain they are "all about customer service," but the second something goes sideways that pledge goes right out the door. Maybe the representative knows all the things that help the company but not necessarily the customer.

This may be why your company is having trouble retaining those customers. We'll talk about retention in more detail later, but this may be a direct result of your customer service reputation. This is a big one. When you are doing customer service right, you should be noticing an influx of referrals coming into your business. Perhaps your company is spending a ton of money on expensive marketing, yet the customers are coming in but going out and never coming back. You want to keep those clients. Some call it client retention. Some people call it client loyalty. I call it creating "raving fan clients" who just can't get enough of you—customers who will write rave reviews online about your customer service. We'll also cover online reviews in this later in this book.

Excellent customer service starts at the top; it starts at the beginning. I believe that poor hiring decisions are at the root of the retention problem. Managers are hiring the wrong personality types to do a very specific job. Companies will hire customer service employees based on their resumes and not their personalities. Oftentimes, managers are hiring people who are egocentric and entitled. One bad apple *can* spoil the whole bunch.

Nepotism can also be a huge problem. I worked with a client—a retail company—that sold natural juice products. I went to their customer service training, and the owner asked me to be a mystery shopper. I went to the location, and the girl who was helping was very rude and nonchalant. She clearly didn't care about me—the customer—one bit. I found out later that this girl was the owner's daughter. There's no incentive to be a terrific employee because she's not afraid of losing her job.

She's probably only there to get by or have something to do. Egocentrism and entitlement are two qualities that are at odds with great customer service.

I also frequently see a lack of leadership and coaching. Here is what I know: Customer service and leadership go hand in hand. Maybe you, as a leader have excellent customer service skills, but you can't impart those skills to your employees— which means it never gets to your customers.

That is why, in this part of the book, we're going to talk a lot about mindset and building that foundation. If you're a manager, a business owner, or a customer service supervisor, I will provide tools to help you influence your team.

Let's focus on leadership right now. What does poor leadership look like? Well, poor communication is one aspect; a lack of consequences for poor customer service is another. On the flip side of this is a lack of reward for excellent customer service. All these can contribute to poor customer service.

I will come in to observe a call center, and management will often tell me, "David, we've got this great incentive going for our employees, but only half of them are excited about it." I always ask, "What's the other side? What are the consequences for not taking advantage of the incentive? You've offered them the carrot. What is the stick?" "We don't really have a stick." People are motivated in different ways. Some want the pleasure the incentive will bring them, while others won't react unless there's a consequence, some sort of loss. For some, a negative response motivates them to do better.

As the leader of a company or customer service department, you have to set clear goals. That vision will establish your values and your mission statement. Some companies might find that their customer service is out of alignment with their goals, values, and mission. That's because the goals aren't being reinforced, leading to guidelines and procedures that don't support their values and mission.

Sometimes, leadership is about recognizing that some employees simply don't have the passion to do the job well or have the passion for customer service specifically. There is no way these employees will deliver that world-class service.

Finally, leaders need to recognize when there's a high level of stress in the workplace that can result in low morale and a poor company culture. Stress kills in many different ways. When we're under pressure or working to hit tough deadlines, employees can't always deliver the best customer service. Isn't that true?

In this program, we're going to learn how to overcome these obstacles. When obstacles are not addressed, the result can be missing those important revenue or commission goals. Some obstacles start with leadership and include managers who don't know how to motivate or coach their employees, which can manifest as a negative impact on the company's bottom line. Another obstacle might be a leader who is afraid of failing, causing stress and low morale among team members. Maybe you're an employee who is at risk of losing your job or a business owner at risk of losing your business. These are all challenges to providing good customer service. Maybe there are some other challenges you're facing that are specific to your business, industry, or customer base that hasn't been addressed. Think about what those things might be, and write them down in a journal. A little later on in this book, I will teach you practical solutions to those challenges.

✶ ✶ ✶

In this section, we're looking at customer service myths. These are the ideas and advice we've been fed for years that just don't work. Here is the one thing that is vital to changing or improving your customer service: growth. Myths can kill growth, and so they must be dispelled in order to enable businesses to move forward. If you want to improve or change your customer service, 80 percent of what's going to help you do that is changing the answers to the "why" questions: Why are we changing our customer service? Why are we improving our customer service? Why are we investing our time and energy and money into providing an excellent customer experience? That final 20 percent is in the answers.

Hopefully, you are continuing to grow and continuing push yourself to be better—just like anybody who's world-class, just like Usain Bolt. When someone is a world-class athlete, do they just stop there? No! They continue to push themselves.

*Myth No. 1: If the company needs my product or service, they will do business with me.*

> ### 85% of customer loss due to poor service was preventable.

In the last section, we talked about what happened after MapQuest was first launched in the '90s. It was a unique tech product among a multitude of unique tech products. The mindset then was that customers who wanted a particular product were going buy said product whether or not the company that sold it provided good customer service.

This is what you need to understand about customer service today: It is six to seven times more expensive to acquire a new customer than it is to keep a current one.

If you don't want to provide great customer service—that's fine. Certainly, there are a lot of companies that are very good at marketing and sales and will make billions of dollars every year from customers coming in the front door and going out the back door. However, if you can close that back door and keep them connected to your company, your company will experience exponential growth—and quickly. Once you get those clients in, you can nurture them and get more clients for free through referrals. It is awesome, and we're going to talk about how to do that in this book.

*Myth No. 2: Customer service is a burden and an expense to your company.*

> Acquiring a new customer is anywhere from five to 25 times more expensive than retaining an existing customer.
> On average, loyal customers are worth up to 10 times as much as their first purchase.

I can't tell you how many call centers I've visited where the management is only worried about getting people on and off the phone quickly because they are paying per minute! Maybe you are doing this to yourself, too, paying per minute for this person to be on the phone. What happens in a situation like is that all the pressure is put on the customer service representative to be quick, which means the customer on the other end may or may not be getting what they need out of that phone call. This also dovetails with what we discussed earlier about personalities. Certain personalities are going to only want to get on the phone and get off. We have all had that one client who just wants to tell you their story and just wants you to listen to them. The thing is, you've got to give them that time even if it feels like an expense to your company. Here is the reality: Nine out of 10 customers would pay more to ensure superior customer experience. *They would pay more.* And companies that deliver excellent customer service can charge 25 percent or more for the same service that their competitors are providing. A perfect example is hotels. When you choose a nice hotel, you're paying more. Why wouldn't pick a cheaper hotel? For the experience! People will pay for the customer service, the architecture, the amenities, the restaurant, the spa, the Jacuzzi—whatever it is. Nine out of 10 people would pay more to ensure a superior customer experience.

*Myth No. 3: We're already providing excellent customer service.*

> 80% of companies say they deliver "superior customer service." 8% of people think these same companies deliver "superior customer service."
> 91% of unhappy customers will not willingly do business with you again.

I love this one—and we have to get honest about it. Here is the reality: 96 percent of your unhappy customers won't tell you they're unhappy. And 91 percent of them simply won't come back. Boom! That's big. If we want to know why, then we must keep this in mind even when we engage them in a survey.

There is one company that I really like. I've gotten great service from them. I am a customer service guy, so I want to give them five stars on their customer service survey. They send me a link, I click on it, and it takes me to a survey that takes 20 minutes to complete. Who's got time for that? Somebody might, but not me. We have to make it easy for customers to engage with us. Whether we are providing excellent customer service or not, we need to make changes to their ability to give us feedback because—remember this—96 percent of unhappy customers won't even tell you they're unhappy and 91 percent simply won't come back.

*Myth No. 4: Customers today are too demanding.*

> **60% of consumers have higher expectations for customer service now than they did just one year ago.**
> **89% of consumers have stopped doing business with a company after experiencing poor customer service.**

As a customer service representative, have you ever had that thought? You know the one; I think we all have at some point: Customers are too demanding. Well, they are—and with good reason. Your customers expect more from you because your competitors are raising the bar every day. You need to keep up or get left behind. Here's an example: coffee in a hotel room. How many of you have ever gone to a hotel room and seen a coffee maker there? I'm on the road quite a bit, and there was a time when that was not the norm. Now, just about every hotel room I stay in has a coffee maker. Why? Because some hotel decided, "Let's get them coffee in their room, and it'll be an *extra* amenity." I'm sure, at the time, there were competitor hotels that thought putting coffee makers in the room was spoiling customers. But now everybody's doing it because that one hotel raised the bar. So, where is the bar being raised in your marketplace right now? You need to make sure that you are up there, too. Your customers aren't too demanding, but they do demand that their favorite brands keep up with that bar.

*Myth No. 5: It is impossible to provide world-class customer service all the time.*

> ### 65% are frustrated by inconsistent experiences across channels.

I hear this from clients a lot—and it is just not true. Does that mean you are going to please everybody all the time? No. But you can provide world-class service all the time. It is like that old saying, you can lead a horse to water but you can't make it drink. You may give customers a world-class service experience, but it doesn't mean they are going to perceive it that way or that they're going to be happy with your service all the time—but that shouldn't stop you from providing your absolute best. That said, with the right strategies and goals in place, you are going to win. I promise.

The eight steps you are going to learn in this book will show you how to deliver that world-class service every day.

*Myth No. 6: Satisfying customers will help us grow our business and create loyal customers.*

> ## 20% of "satisfied" customers intend to leave the company.

I've got bad news for you. That's just not true. Satisfied customers will leave your company for a cheaper brand, a trendy brand or a brand that delivers superior customer service. Satisfied customers don't cut it. But that's what they taught us, right? Make sure your customers are satisfied with your service. Believe it or not, there is a distinct difference between satisfactory and being world-class. Satisfied customers have no loyalty to your brand. Satisfied customers only expect to get the service or product they want when they want it. But that's not what *we* want. What you are going to discover in this book is going to help you and your company to elevate to world-class loyal raving fan clients that will never leave you.

*Myth No. 7: You must wow your customer on every transaction.*

> ## 70% of buying experiences are based on how the customer feels they are being treated. 73% of consumers say friendly customer service reps can make them fall in love with a brand.

Haven't you heard that over the years? "Wow your customers!" I do believe you should do special things for your clients and for your customers to make them feel special, but there's a caveat to that. Wowing your customer on every transaction will give you a headache. How can I outdo the last guy? Wowing your customers is fleeting. Have you ever been to a store or hotel or restaurant, and the staff totally wowed you with its customer service by doing something outstanding? That's great, and you probably still went to a competitor the very next day or next week or next month or next year. The key is relationships. Build relationships with your customers, and you will truly create raving fan clients that will never leave you.

In the last section, we talked about a time when the world was filled with small businesses before the big-box phenomenon took hold of the marketplace. The owners of those small businesses were friends with their customers; they knew their clients on a first-name basis. What if you own or work for a big company? How can you build a relationship with all your clients? The answer is *one client at a time*. You can build a relationship with your clients, and you don't even have to meet them. It's all about making sure your customer service strategy is laid out and locked down in a way that makes doing that possible. Make sense? And—I can't state this enough—doing this will build a raving client base that will never leave you.

*Myth No. 8: It takes a lot of time to provide world-class customer service.*

> 72% blame their bad customer service experience on having to explain their problem to multiple people.

I hear this all the time, especially in call centers. "I just don't have the time to deliver world-class service. I don't have time to do x, y, or z strategy. I'm too busy working." Well, here is the reality: You will actually gain time by providing world-class customer service. How is that possible? It may take a little more time on the front end, but great customer service done right will mean fewer time-consuming mistakes, fewer complaints that you have to deal with, and a cohesive system in place.

So, let's recap the customer service myths—and stop believing them.

★ *If the company needs my product or service, they will do business with me.* That's just not true.

★ *Customer service is a burden and an expense to our company.* Not true. Nine out 10 people would pay more to ensure superior customer service.

★ *We are already providing excellent customer service.* Nope. Actually 96 percent of customers won't tell you they are unhappy and 91 percent won't come back.

★ *Customers are too demanding.* Hardly. More like your competition is raising the bar.

★ *It is impossible to provide world-class customer service all the time.* That's just not true, and this book will give you the skills to do it.

★ *Satisfied customers will help us grow our business and create loyal customers.* It's not satisfied customers but customers who are raving fan clients that you have a relationship with.

★ *You must wow your customer on every transaction.* You *do not* have to do that. Just build relationships, and you will be fine.

★ *It takes a lot of time to provide world-class customer service.* Actually, you will gain time from providing world-class customer service.

---

**45% of customers can't remember having a recent successful customer experience.**

---

This next section focuses on the three customer service states of being. What does that mean? I have taken three different ways of delivering a customer experience and broken them down for you. I am sure you have experienced all three.

The first state of being is called **dark customer service**. What is that? Let me give you an example. I live down by the beach in San Diego, and one night, I wanted Chinese food. I was too lazy to get off the couch, so I went online to look for Chinese food, but it turned out there were not many Chinese delivery places in my area. However, I did finally find a restaurant, so I called them up.

The person on the phone said, "Yeah, we'll take your order."

I said, "I'll get some chicken chow mien."

He replied, "Well, there's a $15 minimum, so you'll have to order something else." I get it: You've got to pay the delivery guy, there's gas, whatever.

"OK. I'll order something else. Give me some wonton soup."

He adds it all up. "That comes to $14.98."

And I'm like, "That's amazing how did we get so close?"

"Well, there's a $15 minimum delivery."

"We're nearly there—$14.98 is awesome!"

He said again, "Well, there's a $15 minimum delivery."

At first, I thought he was kidding around.

I said, "Well, I don't really want anything else. My order is $14.98. We're talking about two cents; don't you think you can deliver anyway?"

"I'm sorry we can't deliver. There's a $15 minimum delivery."

I couldn't believe it. I was steaming mad. This guy just didn't get it. Here's somebody who is the only Chinese delivery in town and could be absolutely crushing it, but we're talking about 2 cents shy of making a delivery. I'm a guy who would probably order from them again and tell my buddies to order from them. The restaurant lost my business in that instant— over 2 cents. This restaurant needed to start thinking about the big picture. And I want you to start thinking about the big picture, too. There are some procedures and policies that might be holding you back from getting that extra business.

Let me tell you what the dark customer service state of being is all about. The people who work in this state of being believe servicing the customers is a waste of money. *A waste of money!* They believe the customer is annoying, the customer is rude, the customer is uneducated, the customer is not worth their time. These companies definitely make a lot of money, but they do so by living in this dark customer service space. Another example: discount airlines. They started in Europe, and there are a couple of them here in the U.S. What they do is offer customers a really low fare, which looks tempting, and they implement a host of crazy terms and conditions, like requiring passengers to print their own tickets. If you don't print out your ticket, they are going to charge you an extra $300–$400. Another one: You can put stuff in your bag, but if your bag doesn't fit because they have smaller carry-on trunk spaces on the airplane, they are going to charge you another $100–$200!

They get the money from you by frustrating you! It's like they're saying, "If we can frustrate them enough we can make enough money and keep on moving." The CEO of one of those companies said, "If our clients are so stupid that they cannot print out their tickets, they deserve to pay more money. F--- them." That's a real quote. I did not make that up! These are business owners who live in that dark, *dark* customer experience—a maze of voice prompts that hang up on customers or encouraging to get help on their website and fan pages. They don't have time to talk to you or email you. They expect you to just go get help on your own. But all you get from them are negative responses or no responses at all! Your issue dies there, and no one from the company calls to make amends or anything. They have policies and procedures that work against customers, but what they need are policies and procedures that are good for the health of the business—but those don't have to be antagonistic toward the customer. Rude customer service representatives are dismissive of the happiness and the well-being of the customer. That's the customer experience over there in the dark. You're just stuck. And when you work at a company like this with these beliefs, you are also stuck! As a customer service representative or a business owner, you feel frustration, and you feel that anxiety. Isn't that true? This dark space is what's causing it.

The next state of being is called **light customer service**. What do they believe? These are companies that believe the customer is always right. They believe the customer is important. They believe the customer should be satisfied. They believe the customer is to be serviced in a timely manner. They believe the customer is worth our time. They believe servicing the customer is expensive, but, hey, it's worth it. I'll give you an example. Not too long ago, I was sitting in front of a red light waiting to make a left turn, and all of a sudden, I see a car coming up behind me. It is moving fast, and it doesn't look like it's going to stop. And it didn't. It just jammed on the brakes and—BOOM!—right into the back of my car. I had to call my insurance company. I don't know if you've ever had to call an insurance company, especially a claims department. They don't always employ the nicest people in the world. In fact, I once had to train some claims department employees, and they just don't have this light customer service mentality all the time. So, I called the client service line, and the lady on the phone was very nice. She took all the information, she put me through the system, and I got the car fixed, and it was a pleasurable experience. This is a good experience of light customer service.

> Customer loss is attributed to the poor quality of customer service.

As a comparison, I bought a house several years ago, and what I didn't know was that it had some faulty plumbing. I hadn't lived there very long when one of the washing machine pipes burst. It was a two-story house, and I had water pouring into my living room downstairs. It was a nightmare. So, I called the homeowners insurance company and spoke with a man in the claims department. This guy treated me like a criminal, like it was my fault, like I had done something wrong. He was rude and getting upset with me, and fighting me on every little part of the claim. As you can see, two totally different experiences. The homeowners insurance company was definitely stuck in the dark, while the car insurance company was a light customer experience—I was a satisfied customer. I pay both of these companies every month, yet only one did the job I pay them to do.

The light customer service state of being means employees keep open communication with customers to solve customer issues as soon as possible. They smile at the customer, they intend to keep wait times low, and they work to solve customer problems. These customer service representatives are knowledgeable about the product or service, and they know what they're talking about. The customer service representatives do the job required effectively and efficiently.

Light and dark states of being might seem like enough, but as I mentioned, there are three customer service states of being. If you can do this third one accurately, you know you are doing customer service right.

The third state of being is called **enlightened customer service**, which states that the customer is our friend, the customer is our guest and our responsibility, the customer deserves to be pampered and feel special, and the customer must always leave happy. Here's the mantra: The customer is everything to our business and servicing the customer is profitable.

I'll give you an example of a company with this philosophy. Not too long ago, my family and I were going to take our kids, the 1-year-old and the 4-year-old, on a skiing trip. They had never seen snow before, so they needed snow suits. We needed the jackets, the puffy pants with the suspenders. We had gone all over San Diego but couldn't find any for toddlers. We looked everywhere. I suggest that my wife go online to see if she could find what we needed. Luckily she did, and they were set to arrive just before we were to leave.

The next day, we get an email. We have a membership account with this particular online retailer. The email said, "The credit card that you had on file is expired." When you are in a membership, there are a lot of different credit cards. My wife accidentally picked the one that had expired. This was an inconvenience but no big deal. They offered an easy fix; we just went into our account, deleted the expired card, and added the new one. After we did that, we were notified that our delivery time was going to change to the day *after* we were to leave. That tiny mistake was going to mess up our delivery. So, I got in touch with customer service, and they were amazing! The gentleman on the phone said, "I understand the problem, and we're going to start working on this for you. I don't want to take too much of your time, so I could send you an email or I could call you back." I said, "Please call us back." A few hours later, he calls me back and says, "I've got great news! We're going to be able to get it to you the day before you leave. We know how important this is for you—that first snow day for your kids."

He added that he would follow up the next day to make sure that it shipped—and that's exactly what happened. This company understood what my needs were as a client. The company made me feel special, and made sure that the problem was fixed and done right. That's enlightened customer service.

When you are an enlightened customer service representative, this is what you want to do to give customers an enlightened experience: You want to use their names. There's nothing we humans like more than to hear our names used by customer service representatives. It makes us feel as if they know us personally. It makes us feel like a rapport has been built—that there is some sort of commonality, some sort of feeling of familiarity that makes us feel cared for. It makes customers or clients feel as though the experience has been custom tailored and personalized for them. The customer service representative is always thinking about how to add extra value to the customer to deepen that relationship. The customers should always be treated with kindness and caring—like a close friend.

Ask yourself: Where are you on this spectrum? Are you in the enlightened category, are you more light customer experience, or are you deep in the dark customer experience? Then ask yourself this very important question: Do you like where you are?

★ ★ ★

In this section, I am going to talk about customer service **SMART goals**. SMART is an acronym, and I will talk about what it stands for in a bit. So far, we have covered the topic of where you are starting from, and we assessed where you are now. We've also talked about where you are headed. We are going to get very specific about what your goals are going to be, and then we are going to fill in the gaps on how to get there. I've worked with customer service clients who have raised their customer service score by 30 percent, blowing away the 20-percent goal we set out to achieve. In order to do that, the company had to know where it was going. I have also worked with clients who have doubled their revenue in six months, but they had to set that goal in order to achieve it. If you are a business owner, what does it mean to you to set smart goals? I could mean you want to get more revenue. If you are a manager, it could mean you want to get high commissions and bonuses; if you are a customer service representative or professional, it could mean you want more money on your paycheck and more opportunity for advancement.

Here's that acronym again: SMART. It defines customer service goals.

The S stands for **Specific**. If you want to achieve a goal, you have to make it specific, and write it down. The simple act of writing it down ensures that you are 400 percent more likely to hit that goal. People have asked me: What does specific mean in this context? How specific should be we? I want your goals to be so specific that if you set this goal and someone from another country came and didn't know what your goal was or didn't know what your business was, they would understand whether or not you hit that goal. That's how specific I want you to be. Maybe it's a survey, or a certain number of referrals, or maybe it's a certain level of client retention (client retention is huge), or maybe it's a revenue goal (an amount to hit in a given span of time).

The second letter is M. Your goal needs to be **Measurable**. Are we getting closer to your goal or moving further away? Is your goal standing still or is it stagnant? Maybe this measurement is a customer service score, or it might be a certain number of referrals, or a certain number of clients who take the time to give your business or customer service staff a compliment or a client testimonial. Whatever it is for you and your business, you need and want it to be measurable.

A stands for **Actionable**. What does that mean? It means something that you can affect, something you and your team can actually impact. There are certain things that you can't impact, like whether or not the sun will rise tomorrow, but there are strategies businesses can put into place that can empower employees to take action, and you want your SMART goals to help achieve that.

Next is R—as in being **Realistic**. I am a coach, so I believe anything is possible, but I really want you to have something that's realistic for you, for your team, and for whatever skill set your team has—something that you can realistically accomplish.

This is especially important for the last letter in this acronym. T stands for **Timeline**. You have to give yourself a timeline to achieve this customer service SMART goal. Why? Do you remember when you were in school you had a report that was due or a test to take on a certain day? You would do whatever it took to get that project done by that day even if you had to stay up until 3 o'clock in the morning the night before. Do you have a timeline now? Timelines provide a sense of urgency and help ensure that you achieve this goal or at least get close.

So, to recap: You want your goal to be **Specific**. You want it to be **Measurable**. You want it to **Actionable**, **Realistic**, and on a **Timeline**. What does that look like? Maybe referrals are a big thing for you and you company. Let's say you set a goal of getting 30 referrals in the next 30 days. Is that goal actionable? Absolutely. And you can positively take specific actions because it is measurable. During those 30 days, you will know if you're getting closer or getting farther away from that goal because you are going to track what's working and what is not working. Is it realistic? Absolutely. And it's on a timeline—30 days. It's very important that all of these elements are there— every single one of them—when you are putting together your customer service SMART goal.

★ ★ ★

Congratulations! You have gotten through Chapter 1. High five! Boom!

Let's do a recap before we get down to the nitty-gritty in the upcoming chapters.

First, we looked at the challenges you and your company may be facing. We looked at why it is so hard to find excellent world-class service these days and what happens when customer service is not world-class.

We also looked at the old-school customer service versus the new school—the customer service timeline.

Then we examined the eight myths companies and individuals get sucked into believing, and we also delved into the three customer service states of being: the dark, the light, and the enlightened. Lastly, we went over customer service SMART goals.

This is your foundation. It will be important in the upcoming chapters to consider the following questions and ideas:

What does world-class service mean to you? You may want to recall a time when you experienced excellent customer service, an example that really sticks out in your mind. How were you treated by a representative? How did that company's product make you feel? How did the people make you feel?

Where is your company's customer service state of being at right now? What is your state of being as a representative? Be honest with yourself: Are you in the dark, are you in the light, or are you enlightened?

On a scale from 1 to 10, rate your company's customer service. If it is less than 10, write down what would make it a 10.

Create a compelling SMART goal that you are committed to achieving. Get it really clear in your head, and follow the SMART guidelines.

What are the top three challenges that could prevent you from achieving your SMART goal? It will be important as we go through the rest of the book to be thinking about these challenges—how they pop up and how you are going to overcome them. I am going to give you a ton of tools, and you could choose one of them or all of them to overcome those challenges—depending on your needs.

Now, let's get to work.

*"Every great business is built on friendship."*

—JAMES CASH PENNEY, JR., FOUNDER JCPENNEY

*"We see our customers as invited guests to a party, and we are the hosts. It's our job every day to make every important aspect of the customer experience a little bit better."*

—JEFF BEZOS, CEO OF AMAZON

# ★ 2

# GET LEVERAGE

Welcome to Secret No. 2. We are going to start the second chapter with something I call "getting leverage." You have to get leverage for yourself, for your company, and your employees. What do we mean by getting leverage? A lot of times, when you want to take your company to the next level, it involves a change of some sort. One needs to experience some kind of growth in order to move the needle—that could be learning new skills or getting better at the skills you have, and learning different mindsets. When we do that, our brains will often tell us, "Hey, if I am going to change something, it better be worth it for me to follow through."

Have you ever been to a seminar, or read a book, or got some great information or a wonderful idea that you knew if you tried any of it, it would change your business—or maybe even your life—but then you didn't implement it? Why not? In a bit, I'm going to answer that question with some brain science, but briefly, on a surface level, our brains don't like change. We like our habits, we like patterns, and we like to know what's coming next. Whenever a person wants to change something, they need to have a big enough reason to want to change. When I didn't have any referrals coming in for my entertainment company business, I needed to crack that code as soon as possible or I wouldn't have a company anymore. That is leverage. I needed to change, grow, add news skills, etc.

I'll give you another great example. There's a rental car company—one of the biggest privately held companies in the world—and the only way to get promoted or to get acknowledged for pay raises is to get good customer service ratings. That's how the company was built, and that's how it grew: The company put all the focus on the customer. The company also empowered its employees to give upgrades, to offer discounts—it basically allowed them to do whatever it would take within reason to keep the customer happy. When you have those kinds of employee policies in place and provide the right training—that's leverage. The employees are embedded. It is part of the culture. Your clients are happy, your employees are happy, and now everyone's on the same page—it all works out. When your company mindset is that customers come first and customers are No. 1., and you've got the strategies to back that up, everything moves forward.

I will tell you another truth about leverage. Anything you have ever wanted and achieved in life, you had a compelling *why* behind it.

Several years ago, I wanted to audition for *Survivor*. I'm an adventurous guy, and when the TV show first aired, I knew I could do it. And I actually got an opportunity to audition for the show—but there's more to this story. At the time, I also was an avid motorcycle rider. I would go out on the track and drag my knee around the corners. It's such a great experience. I love the adrenaline boost. About this time, I had bought some new tires for my bike from some guy at the track—so I didn't actually know how new they were. I was riding my bike at the track one day, and the tires kept slipping.

When you ride a motorcycle around a track, the tires will get sticky over time, and that helps the bike stick to the track. These kept slipping out. So, picture this: I'm coming around this corner at 90 miles an hour, coming in straight, and my tires slipped out from under me. The tires kept spinning, and I flipped over like a mouse trap. In motorcycle riding, we call it a "high side." I was wearing a helmet, my leather, and some Kevlar, so I thought I was protected, but I landed on my shoulder and dislocated it, and I broke my wrist and my foot. As I was thrown off of the motorcycle, my motorcycle was barreling at me at 90 miles an hour. It was lights out! When I woke up, I was in an ambulance. I didn't know how I got there or even who I was. It's funny the things you do remember in times of trauma: I could remember my mom's cell phone number. I told the paramedic that he should call my mom and tell her not to worry, that I'd had a "little" accident.

I survived, and I was still in the healing process, so, of course, *this was the moment* I got the opportunity to go to *Survivor*. I couldn't even do a pushup because of my wrist had been fractured. My shoulder was still in pain and so was my foot. But I *really* wanted to be on the show—and that was the leverage for me. I hired a personal trainer, a buddy of mine and a trainer to the stars. I told him, "Hey, you have got to get me in shape in time so that I can be good for this audition, so I can go on this adventure, this dream of mine." I went through it with him, and, boy, did I ever push myself. I got in great shape, probably the best I've ever been in my life. Regrettably, because my bones didn't heal as fast as the rest of my body, I wasn't able to go on the show that season. But what ended up happening was that I started to build a new habit—a new habit of fitness, of health—and that was the leverage that got me to move. All it took was trying to get on *Survivor*.

The point of this anecdote is this: If there is something you want badly enough, you are going to do whatever it takes to get it. So, your job now is to find the leverage that will take your customer service to the next level and make it world-class. If you are already world-class, you need to find that leverage that will motivate you to continue to stay at that world-class level and crush your competitors. That's what you are supposed to do; that's what you are *going* to do.

> 62% of customer service organizations view customer experience as a competitive differentiator.
> Poor customer service experience has motivated 62% of global consumers to avoid a brand or company.

In this next section, we're going to examine the five pillars that explain why customer service is important.

"But David," you're thinking, "we already get it. Customer service is important. That's why I'm reading this book." I hear you, but I want to connect your brains specifically to the reasons why customer service is so important for *you*. This is really important, because those reasons need to be reinforced, you need to know them intellectually, and they need to be ingrained in your mind. These pillars need to be almost like a part of your nervous system. You need to follow through on all these skills, and you have to go through the steps to make sure you get it, feel it, and live it every day. Here are the five pillars:

*"When you dedicate additional minutes to solve your customer's problem on the front end, you can gain valuable hours for yourself on the back end."—David Brownlee*

*1. Providing world-class service helps you gain time.*

I can't tell you how many clients tell me, "David, I don't have time to implement excellent customer service and work with my team on all these different things." I tell them, "It will help you gain time." How? It will help cut down on customer complaints. When you get things right the first time, there will be fewer customer complaints. When you get things right the first time, you won't be running around trying to fix internal things that aren't even the customer's problem. You gain time that way. You gain time from having strategies in place so the work runs efficiently, so you are not making decisions on the fly all the time. If you provide world-class service, you will gain time to continue doing it.

> "The goal as a company is to have
> customer service that is not just
> the best, but legendary."
> —Sam Walton

*2. Customer service is the best way to distinguish your business from the competition.*

A lot of products nowadays have similar quality and pricing—particularly electronics. Those big-box stores sell the same brands with the same pricing, so what makes one stand out over the other? What if you are a medium-sized company or a mom-and-pop shop trying to compete with those guys? Customer service will help you distinguish your business because that's the one trait those big-box competitors cannot imitate even if they try. It is something that's in your organization. It is something that's in you, and that's going to help you stand out. That is what this book is designed to help you do.

> "Every company's greatest assets
> are its customers, because without
> customers there is no company."
> —Michael LeBoeuf, author

*3. Customers are everything to your business.*

Customers allow your business to exist. Simply put: No customers, no business! As a customer service representative, you have to really connect in your brain that these clients are putting food on your table. They are helping you pay your rent, they are helping you pay your mortgage or your car payments, and they are helping put your kids through school. All of those things hinge on the customer. It is important to know this if you have a difficult customer, isn't it? You may be at your wit's end with this person, but remember that this customer is your livelihood. Say it again: Customers are your livelihood. It's imperative to remember how important they are and connect it with your brain. Even if they are having a bad day, they allow your business to exist.

> "Loyal customers, they don't just come back,
> they don't simply recommend you, they insist
> that their friends do business with you."
> —Chip Bell, author

*4. You have to provide world-class customer service because it will help build customer loyalty and retention.*

Remember what I taught you earlier in the book: It is six to seven times more expensive to bring in a new customer than to keep the one you already have. When you keep clients happy, when you bring out new products and new services, or provide a recurring product or service, you will find that you can sell it to them over and over again. And when you are providing them world-class service, guess what? They are going to tell their friends or a co-worker or a family member, and they're going to start bringing in business. "Oh, you've *got* to come to this business!" they'll say. Loyalty and retention are going to help build your customer database, expand it, and help your company grow and increase revenue. This inevitably pays dividends to you: When your business is growing, there is more opportunity for you, for advancement, for pay raises. Everything is interconnected.

> "If you make customers unhappy in the physical world, they might each tell six friends. If you make customers unhappy on the Internet, they can each tell 6,000."
> —Jeff Bezos

*5. Review sites are everywhere!*

Do you use any review sites? I bet you do. For travel, restaurants, or hotels, products—something. Review sites will show you how many stars that business or service has received—ratings given to them by the public. I do a lot of traveling all around the world for speaking engagements. If I am in a new city and want to head out to dinner, I am not going to risk missing an appearance because of food poisoning. I will check one of these review sites on my phone or computer, search for different restaurants, and I'll look at how many stars they have for their overall rating. My cutoff is 3.5 stars (though, frankly, I prefer 4 or 5). It doesn't matter if you are a restaurant or a tire company. If you own a business with fewer stars than that, I am not picking your establishment for my business! Potential customers can now go online, see your reviews, and instantly make that crucial decision about whether or not they want to give you a shot. That's big! Before review sites, if you experienced great customer service, you might tell three of your friends. That was the reach of your referral. If your customer service experience was bad, you might tell as many as nine people. Now, if you go on a review site, and you submit a review or someone else submits one, that review—positive or negative—can reach an audience of thousands or even millions of potential customers depending on the size of your business. You need to make sure you are doing everything you can to get as many good ratings as you can by implementing that world-class and excellent customer service.

> Consumers are two times more likely to share their bad customer service experiences than they are to talk about positive experiences.

A few years back, I went on vacation to Playa del Carmen in the Mexican Riviera with my wife and a bunch of friends. This place just screams vacation: white sand beaches, the aqua crystal-clear water, palm trees, the music, the atmosphere, and the enticing smell of barbeque is everywhere. It is just amazing. On our first night there, we went looking for a place to get dinner. In Playa del Carmen, when you walk into town, there's a main drag with hundreds of restaurants from side to side. It's only a few miles long, but there are restaurants everywhere. We see one restaurant that looks great. There's some music going on in there, and it is packed. We immediately want to go in there, but I say, "Whoa! Let's check out our international app and see what kind of rating it has." Turns out, the rating was only two stars, and it said "horrible food, bad service." It may or may not have been true, but guess what? We kept walking. We checked the app again and found another place with music that had 5 stars. We had a great time, an excellent meal, and great service—and that's the way it went.

If you are rated and reviewed online, you have to ask yourselves if you are happy with what people are saying. A lot of the time I talk with business owners and they say, "Yeah, well, this person said they had this problem, and this one had that problem—and it is not really fair because we are better than that." Remember we talked about getting honest? You have to ask yourself if you really *are* better than that or if these customers pinpointed a problem that maybe you never noticed or are ignoring. On the flip side, you may have five-star reviews. Great. You are providing excellent customer service, world-class. Now, the question is: How do you stay there? You want to be thinking about these things constantly, because quality doesn't stand still. What worked for you yesterday might not work for you today, especially because of how rapidly technology changes. It is changing every marketplace and industry. Customer service is no different—it is continually changing.

Here is a quick recap of the five pillars that explain why customer service is important:

★ Providing world-class customer service helps you gain time. We are going to talk much more about that to get you in that mindset.

★ Customer service is the best way to distinguish your business from its competitors. It doesn't matter what industry you're in, great customer service is something that is very hard for people to duplicate, and it will help you and your business stand out.

★ Customers are everything to your business. They allow your business to exist.

★ When you provide excellent customer service that is world-class, you build loyal customers and you retain those customers—those raving fan clients that we are looking for.

★ Review sites are everywhere, so you have to get it right.

I'll share one more story with you to really drive the point home. There is a sushi restaurant not too far from my house. I go there often with my wife and kids because we enjoy this place a lot. It's is called Fish Attack—weird name, great sushi. We go in there month after month after month, and they get hundreds of my dollars, maybe even thousands. One night, we went there for dinner, and I ordered a tuna roll. But something was off—the color was off a little bit, and it didn't taste right. I wasn't about to risk getting sick, so I politely sent it back. I even felt bad about doing it. The server who took our order looked at me and said, "Well, you know you've got to pay for it anyway." I said, "Why do I have to pay for it? Something is off, something is wrong with it." And she just got angrier. She said again, "No, you've got to pay for it." This was outrageous. The woman was going on and on and on, and finally she said, "If you don't pay for it, I'm calling the police!" Call the police over sushi rolls? WOW!

> **82% of consumers have stopped doing business with a company because of bad customer service.**

When we look at dark, light, and enlightened customer service, where does this incident fall in that spectrum? Pretty obvious, right? The server was way over on the dark side. I don't know what was going on with her that day or what was happening at the restaurant, but she kept yelling about calling the cops. I didn't want to make a bigger scene than the one that was already in progress, so I agreed to pay the bill—and she still angrily stormed away. I was stunned. She took the whole incident so personally. She claimed she was the owner of the restaurant, but I didn't believe her. It was a horrible customer experience that left a bad taste in my mouth—literally and figuratively. The server came back with the bill and said, "I'll let you go this time, but don't ever do it again." "Do it again?" I asked. "Do you think I'm ever coming back here? You've got to be kidding me!"

I left the restaurant with my family and immediately got on my cell phone, launched one of my favorite review apps, and proceeded to give this place one star. I wrote a review in which I said that if the app would allow me to give this place zero stars or negative stars, I would. This particular app does allow other people to interact with you, and someone said to me that they had the exact same experience. Overall, they have a good rating because the sushi is really good. But I am never going back there again. Instead of Fish Attack, they should rename it Human Attack!

I cannot stress how important good service is. It really does matter to you and your bottom line. We all have had experiences like this. Take a moment and ask yourself: Why is customer service—and providing a world-class experience—so important? Because it has to resonate with you.

✶ ✶ ✶

In this section, we are going to continue talking about the benefits of providing world-class service—but I will be focusing specifically on the benefits to the customer service professional. It is so important to really connect these benefits to your personal well-being. Why? You may be dealing with irate customers all day or tight deadlines and other work pressures that might affect your attitude and mood. In moments of stress, your representative, your company, or you yourself may be interacting with a customer—and that customer doesn't care about what's bothering you—he or she still expects excellent customer service. You will find that when you can focus on the customer and deliver a world-class experience, your personal morale and mood will actually improve.

There are two types of customers: The first are external customers. These are vendors and/or people buying your products or services. The second are internal customers. These are your co-workers, or management, or leadership, or the employees who work for you. Internal relationships are very important to maintain. When we talk about delivering world-class service, it includes delivering world-class service to each other. Why? When there are more smiles in the office, everyone is happier. Happier employees, happier customers, and happier you result in more advancement opportunities, pay raises, recognition and acknowledgement, and more opportunities to grow. Trust me on this: It's the trickle-down theory. That good energy will come through to customers, your vendors, and each other. It is important for you to see the benefits of providing that world-class customer service, not only to customers, but to each other as well. We will take a deeper dive into this subject later in the book.

Let's recap. The benefits of providing world-class service to the customer service professional specifically include: better morale; closer relationships with customers, co-workers, and management; more opportunities for advancement, pay raises, recognition, and growth!

✳ ✳ ✳

> **81% of companies with strong capabilities and competencies for delivering excellent customer experiences are outperforming their competition.**

We're now going to delve into the benefits of providing world-class customer service as it pertains to your company.

The first one is business growth. When you provide world-class customer service—and you're doing it right—your business will grow. As business grows, you gain more customers who will bring their business to you more often. Here's the kicker: Now that you are providing world-class customer service, you can begin to charge 25 percent more than your competitors because you have gained the loyalty of your customer base. You are charging more, revenue is going up—and now you have more people to sell to. Call it client retention, client loyalty, what you have developed is a base of raving fan clients that will never leave you. Now you have people who are going to tell other people how great you are.

What about online? It doesn't matter if you are a tech company or an online company, most people now being their searches for products and services online, right? Of course. And review sites have such powerful search engine optimization (SEO) capabilities that, in some cases, the review site will come up higher in searches before your own company website. This is incredibly important because it means that a potential client will see the reviews of your company first. If you have 5 stars, 4 stars, 4.5 stars, then you will attract more clients online because you look great. Remember the example I gave about when I'm traveling? If you are a business that's rated 3 stars, I am passing you by. So, good customer service that results in good reviews online can increase your online revenue, too. People will click on your website next.

This is almost like free advertising. I have said this several times so far in this book—because I can't reiterate it enough—*it is six to seven times more expensive to attract a new customer than it is to keep the ones you already have*. When you can save money, grow your business, increase your revenue, get more online clients, and build those raving fan clients that are never going to leave you, you are in a great spot.

We have reached the end of the topic of getting leverage. And we're going to continue to take an even deeper look at how leverage helps you provide world-class customer service. But what are the takeaways from this chapter?

Customers want to enjoy a special experience, and that's what you want them to have. You want them to feel good, and you need them to associate feeling good to you and your company. You want them to experience this in their minds, in their bodies, in their emotions—happiness, joy, enthusiasm, passion, and maybe even love for your company. All these things help build these raving fan clients that never leave you.

> News of bad customer service reaches more than twice as many ears as praise for a good service experience.

You want to make sure your clients are feeling three very specific ways after their interactions with you and your company.

**Heard.** When they are upset or have a problem with customer service or a product, you must show them that you're listening to them.

**Understood.** It's not enough to listen. You must also show that you understand them. Understanding the problem is a huge part of making a client happy, and we will delve into that more deeply later in the book.

**Cared for.** You've got to make sure the client or customer has been taken care of and that he or she feels like you have taken care of them—because they are going to share their experience with their families and friends just like you would when you experience something great. For example, when you see a great movie, what's the first thing you want to do? You want to tell your friends because you want them to experience that same joy.

A customer who feels all three of these things after an interaction with you or your company is really important because it will reap benefits. Before we move on to the next chapter, I want you to think about what those benefits are for you. What resonates with you, your team, and your brand? Make sure you've got that clearly in mind, make sure it is big, and make sure it is compelling. If you know all the reasons why you are going to deliver world-class customer service, you will deliver it. Next, I want you to write down what resonates with you and why customer service is important to you. If you are going to provide world-class customer service, what benefits will you get? By writing it down, you will really connect with your reasons for providing world-class customer service.

Think of a time when you had horrible customer service. What made it horrible? How did it make you feel? Think of a time you had excellent customer service. What made it excellent? How did that make you feel?

If your company has been delivering less than a 10 in customer service, how is that impacting your company in time, money, resources, etc.?

If you do not improve your customer service now, what will it cost your company in the future?

When you do improve your customer service, what benefits will you, your company, and your customers experience?

The answers to these questions will really make it real for you and connect your brain and your emotions to why you want to deliver excellent customer service.

*"People do not follow leaders, they follow the values and beliefs that the leader stands for."*

—DAVID BROWNLEE

*"Businesses often forget about the culture, and ultimately, they suffer for it because you can't deliver good service from unhappy employees."*

—TONY HSIEH, CEO OF ZAPPOS

CHAPTER

3

# PSYCHOLOGY IN CUSTOMER SERVICE

n this chapter, we're going to dive into Secret No. 3: psychology in customer service. I'd like to start with a story. I call it "First Class Versus No Class." I fly a lot, and I have crazy experiences from both sides of the customer service spectrum. I recently had a speaking engagement in Miami, and it was awesome! I was flying first class—and let me tell you, the airlines really take good care of you. I had glassware, there was a tablecloth—I even had a *real knife* in first class. It was practically fine dining, and it was amazing. I even had one of those massage chairs with the rollers in them that go up and down your body. My whole airplane seat could recline like a bed. The service was simply impeccable. "Is there anything else you need, Mr. Brownlee?" They knew my name. Very, very cool.

But I have a family, so when I travel with my wife and my two young children, we're not usually flying first class. What's the difference between first class and coach? A lot. Besides first class being located in the front of the plane and economy or coach being in the back—usually separated by a thin little curtain—the two parts of the plane are separated by a mindset. The customers are treated very differently even though it's the same plane, same passenger, same airline. And that may be by design. That mindset might trickle down through the company from the top—all the way down to the flight attendants. But as I said, that could be by design. We'll talk more about your company's philosophy and how it trickles down to your employees and customers little later in this chapter.

I once traveled with my family to Europe. Typically, we are allowed to board the plane ahead of other passengers because we have strollers and carry-on bags, etc. On this flight, even though we were boarding together (and boarding first), we didn't have our seats together. At the time, we had a 1-year-old and a 3-year-old, and I wasn't going to let my children sit by themselves. I could see two flight attendants standing in the plane chatting with one another and having fun. I walked up and said, "Excuse me, we don't have our seats together. I wondered if you could help us find some seats all together?" One of the flight attendants looked at me and said, "Well, I don't see anyone else on the plane yet so there's no one else to ask!" I was like, "OK, cool. Can you help us out when more people board the plane?" The other flight attendant looked at me and said, "Well, you can do it yourself." *Uh, OK.* Can you imagine? Here are two flight attendants seemingly in good spirits around each other, but when the customer is there, their attitude changes and the quality of service changes with it.

> **It takes 12 positive customer experiences to make up for one negative experience.**

Here's the problem: More and more of us are working in high-stress environments now, aren't we? Air travel, specifically, is one of the worst for passengers and employees. Everyone is under a tremendous amount of pressure. When we're stressed, we won't always react positively to internal or external customers. Internal customers, if you recall from the last chapter, are the people we work with in our office, our management, our leadership; our external customers are our vendors, our clients, our customers. Sometimes, our personal lives can spill over into our professional lives—relationship difficulties, financial challenges, health issues, etc. When this happens, we may have moments when we don't treat our customers the way they deserve to be treated—with kindness and caring. This can create additional friction when customers or clients are also upset and/or managing stress in their own lives. When these two things collide, we have to figure out how to manage our emotions and actions because everyone has a personal life.

Most people go through their lives at the mercy of circumstance. When something good happens to you, you feel good; if something bad happens to you, you feel bad until something good happens again. Do you know someone like that, maybe intimately? Here's the thing, it's natural for a person to continue to feel bad until something good happens to them. We've all experienced that ourselves or know someone who has.

This section of the book deals with the importance of managing your attitude and your emotions, and how to manage them at will. You might be thinking, "David, that's impossible!" It *is* possible, and it is also super simple, easy, and fast. I'm going to show you how to do it. You'll be able to give world-class customer service to every customer regardless of what's going on in your life, regardless of something good or something bad that has happened. This is the foundation—and this is a long chapter, so buckle up and sharpen your pencil. We're going to get through this together. It will be worth it!

This chapter will teach you to build the foundation for delivering world-class customer service by starting with your psychology. Let's start with the definition of psychology. Psychology is the mental or behavioral characteristics of an individual or a group—and it accounts for 80 percent of your success in taking your customer service to the next level, which is why I'm going to spend a lot of this book going over it.

Why is psychology so important? Have you ever been to a seminar, read a book, taken a class, learned something new—maybe online—or had an idea that could really transform your business or even transform your life, but you didn't implement it? Have you ever attended a weekend seminar that breathed life back into the start of your new work-week? In some fashion, this has probably happened to all of us. It all has to do with our psychology, and we're going to go deep into that so that you can control it and make sure that after reading this book, you and your team members will be able to implement psychological tools that will help you get results—because that's what matters.

We're going to look at psychology in customer service from three vantage points.

*1. The psychology of your company*—because it all starts with the company. *2. The psychology of your customers.* What do they want? What do they expect from you? How do their brains work when you're presenting your product or customer service solution? *3. The psychology of you.* How do you control your emotions and your attitude? How do you make sure you're playing at level 10 every day? If you're a sports fan, or a music fan, or a film and theater fan, or fan of anyone who is world-class at what they do, you know that when they step out on that stage or field, they have to be performing at 10 or higher, don't they? Absolutely. It's the same with you and your business. If you're a business owner, when you step into that office—that is your stage, and you need to be operating at 10. It's the same if you're a manager or executive, or a customer service representative. You need to be the best. And you're about to learn how. So, let's dive in!

> **A 5% increase in customer retention levels result in a 75% increase in the value of the company.**

Let's start with the psychology of your company, because this is where the heart of your customer service starts. What is the mindset of your company? What are its values and its mission statement? What is the company culture? What are its policies and procedures? Your customer service strategy must be focused on providing world-class customer service, and so the implementation of that strategy must be in alignment with the culture. If everything is aligned, those causes and effects will trickle down to your customers. When it's out of alignment, all the negative effects of that misalignment will *also* trickle down to your customers. This is super important: If you work for a company that doesn't have a mission or doesn't have values—or maybe they do, but they have nothing to do with customer service—then, in this section, you'll get a chance to craft some core values, maybe five to 10, that are important to you personally as well as values that are important to your company and what you want your customers to experience. Here's why that's so important. When your core values are in alignment with your personal values, you are more likely to follow through on those customer service strategies. If they're out of alignment—if your company believes one thing and you believe another—how likely are you to deliver great customer service? If you don't believe in the company's philosophy, if you don't believe in the policies or the procedures, that can't happen. Everything has to be in alignment from the top down.

There is an online shoe company that I love. The brand started as a little shoe company, and now they are a multi-billion-dollar company. They're definitely doing something right. The standard operating procedure of the company is to build the brand on extraordinary customer service—world-class. It's so good that what happened next is almost unbelievable. The founder and CEO of the company was out partying in L.A. with some clients and friends, and one of the revelers that night, a woman who had been drinking, said, "I'm hungry. I want a pizza." She says, "I am going to call my shoe company rep and have him get me a pizza." Here's the best part: Her "shoe company rep" worked for the company where this guy was the CEO and founder. She didn't recognize him and didn't know she was partying with him. So, she calls up the rep and says, "Hey, what's up? I want a pizza." The rep goes along with it. "Hey! How are you doing?" he said. "You want a pizza? Where are you?" She gives the rep her address and her order. He asks, "Do you want me to use your card?" She says, "Yeah, that's great," and hangs up the phone.

How did the CEO react knowing that somebody just called his shoe company and had a rep order a pizza? He was proud. He was like a proud papa, because that's the culture he wanted to create with his company. He wanted his company to be so good at customer service that somebody would call his company to order a pizza. And it gets even better. This company sells lots of products now, but if you call looking for a pair of shoes, and those shoes are out of stock, that customer service rep is empowered to sell another pair of shoes from a competitor. They will pay for them, ship them, and send them to your house. That is big! That is so big. We're going to talk more about this shoe company later on in this book.

On the flip side, I usually rent from one particular rental car company. My family and I were going on vacation. My wife found a package deal that included a rental car from a company in L.A. that I hadn't heard of. It was right by the airport in a huge rental center, and we waited in a long winding line—you know those lines. We might as well have been waiting for a ride at Disneyland. As we were standing in line, I noticed that there were about 10 representatives up front and a big sign above them that says, "Miles of Smiles," That's the motto of this company. Being a customer service guy, I really like that. "Miles of Smiles" is awesome. I looked over to check out the rental car agents. Guess how many were smiling? Zero! Not one. So, here's an example of a company with a mantra or mission statement that describes its core value, but it is way out of alignment with the experience. Your company values and mission also must be in alignment with the policies and procedures. If you're telling the world, "We love our customers!" but then, when you actually deal with a customer, you tell them that they are exempt from this deal or that a particular policy doesn't apply to the current transaction, etcetera, etcetera, all that's going to do to is frustrate them.

Customer service must be in alignment with your policies and procedures. This is particularly important if you're a manager or an owner. If you're the leader in your organization, you have to lead it with kindness and caring. This includes clearly communicating the mission, the policies, and the procedures, because that will get you buy-in from your staff and team members. If you're telling your employees that they have to give excellent customer service to your clients, but you're not treating the people who are tasked with executing that service with that same kindness and caring, what are the odds that they are going to treat customers with kindness and caring? That goes for your personal behavior as well. Have you ever thought about that? If you're getting pressure from shareholders or company executives, and you're taking out that frustration on your team, I guarantee your team will not deliver excellent customer service. It starts with you and your relationship with your internal customers, the people who you work with, the people who you support, the people who you're coaching and leading every day. And, finally, if the company and management are not bolstering the integrity of the values and the mission, the negative effects of that are going to trickle down to the customers. Make sense?

✳ ✳ ✳

In the last section, we talked about the psychology of your company. In this section, we're going to talk about the psychology of your customers, your clients and, your vendors as well as your internal customers—your co-workers, the people you lead, the people you manage, or the people you look up to.

When you get to the heart of the psychology of customer service, it's important to remember that there are only three things a customer wants from you and your company. Just three things. You are probably thinking, "Come on, David! What are you talking about? I can make a whole laundry list of things that customers want." When you break it down to these three things, it will make customer service a lot simpler.

*1. Customers want to be **heard**.* When working with customers, representatives should be talking 20 percent of the time and listening other 80 percent. When we listen, we get the information we need to best service that client.

*2. Customers want to be **understood**.* Have you ever had a conversation with a customer service rep and you just feel like the rep is responding to you in a way that has nothing to do with that problem? That's because they don't understand you or the problem you're experiencing with a product or service—and that can be frustrating.

*3. Customers want to be **cared for**.* When you feel cared for, you feel special, don't you? Of course! You feel significant, and that's a human need that we all have.

Here's an example. A while back, I was writing a book, and I wanted some peace and quiet. I rented a cottage way up in the mountains with nobody around on a little ranch in the mountains of California—literally in the middle of nowhere. I get there, and the place was just a perfect sanctuary to get creative—and that's what I was looking for. In fact, it was near a horse dealer, so my only neighbor was a beautiful horse. It was such a peaceful experience, and I was certain I was going to get a lot done.

A little background on my writing process: First, I like to journal and get the ideas out of my head, and then put them on paper. Then I do my research. I love getting into this part of the process. I also write the journal entries into documents and save them on the computer.

I had gotten some of that done when all of a sudden these weird lines began to appear on the computer screen. Oh, no! What's going on? Next thing I know, the computer dies. This can't be happening, I think. I came here to this cabin to write.

And of course, this happened over a weekend. I didn't know what to do. So, I turned the computer off, went back to writing in the journal, and getting my ideas down. Later, I tried turning on the computer again. Luckily, the work I had done had been saved. So, I started the process of transferring the new notes from my journal to the computer—and the trouble started again, the lines began appearing. A few minutes later— boom! It dies. Now the computer is fatally dead. I can't revive it. There's nothing else I can do.

The next part of this story is something I will never forget. I knew that I wouldn't be able to do anything that day because the computer company's business center isn't open on the weekend. So, I called the company that Monday and got Gaby on the phone. She was so great. She listened to everything I was saying. She really heard me. I could tell she really understood my frustration and understood that this book was important to me. She's says, "Oh my gosh! You're way out there. Let me see where the nearest center is where they can fix your computer." She's looking and looking, and after a few minutes, she says, "Go to this place. It's an hour and a half away from you. We can take a look at your computer or we can get you another one." She really made me feel cared for and made me feel special. In the end, I decided to keep journaling rather than go to the computer center near the cabin. I ended up going to the computer center by my house. But Gaby nailed *all three things* that I listed earlier in this section, the things that customers want from customer service representatives: She listened. She understood. She cared.

You must break down customer service into these three elements. If you can make your clients and your customers feel heard, understood, and cared for, then you are delivering world-class service. This part is so important.

*It's the key.*

Let's say it again: Customers want to be heard, understood, and cared for. That's how our brains work. That's how we're wired as humans, and when you can meet those needs, now you're cooking with gas.

✷ ✷ ✷

The previous section was about the psychology of your customers. In this section, we're going to talk about the psychology of *you*! You are where it all starts. We're going to talk about your brain. This isn't a complete course on how your brain works, but I will give you a little glimpse into the topic because it is another passion of mine—studying the brain, how it works, and how we do what we do. I'm going to give you the foundation. Excellent customer service starts with a positive attitude, but everything that happens in our personal lives—the pressures at work, angry customers—can make it hard for us to keep it all together. In this part of the book, I'm going to teach you exactly what to do so that you can control your emotions.

Your brain—this little three-pound computer genius inside your head—doesn't come with a user manual. But I can tell you what it's wired for. It is wired for survival. Everything it does is designed to protect you and keep you alive. Your subconscious is inside your head, and it keeps you breathing, and pumping blood through your veins. That's its only job, its only function. We know the brain can do a lot more than that—and it does—but that's its main function.

Have you ever tried to change a habit, but it just didn't work? Why not? It's because change can mean pain, especially if it's something that you've tried before and it didn't work out—like a diet or a new business or a relationship. Your brain will sabotage your efforts through procrastination, or lack of willpower, or create excuses for why you can't change whatever it is you're trying to change. This is your brain's way of sparing you from pain. Your brain knows that too much pain means death—even if the result would bring you pleasure. We'll discuss that more in detail in a bit.

There's a part of the brain called the amygdala, and it's responsible for subconscious decisions designed keep you safe. If you experience pain and failure, your brain does not like it. However, when you set a positive goal for yourself and visualize that goal, your brain releases a chemical—dopamine, a feel-good chemical. You don't need to smoke anything to get this good feeling; it is already inside you. That's why, when you visualize something you really want and you focus on it with all your intentions, you feel good because your brain is releasing that dopamine.

The brain also produces a chemical called oxytocin. This chemical gets released when you share something positive with another person, a loved one, or even a team. Oxytocin is often called the "love chemical" because it also brings you pleasure when people connect, and it acts as a natural morphine. When women give birth naturally, their bodies produce oxytocin. It is our body's natural way of creating pleasure chemicals.

This is a lot of information about chemicals, and you may

be wondering how it all relates to delivering world-class customer service. When you're not in a positive state of mind or you're feeling unsatisfied or just lousy, you will transfer those feelings directly to your customers. In turn, they will feel lousy, and they will associate feeling lousy with doing business with you and your company. On the flip side, when you're feeling positive and happy, you will transfer those emotions to your customers, and they'll associate your business with a happy and positive feeling.

The next question is the obvious one: How do you control your emotions and your attitudes—especially if things are going wrong?

We're going to get into some techniques for how to do that, but first I want to share a story with you. I'm a big skier and snowboarder. I've been doing it for 30 years. For the past few years, I've been going with a few buddies up to the mountains in California, in the Sierras. During one trip there several years ago, I rented some skis. The rental guy asked me if I was a beginner, intermediate, or advanced skier. I said, "Well, I'm advanced." If you're a skier, and you tell somebody you're advanced, they will crank down what's called bindings. Skiing can be an aggressive sport. Skiers might take a lot of jumps or ski through deep powder, so you put your foot in the ski boot, your ski boot goes into these bindings, and it locks you in. Keep this in mind. So, now my buddies and I go up to the top of the mountain, we're skiing and having a great time. We get up toward the top of the mountain, there's a lot of powder, and we're doing a very simple maneuver—just traversing the mountain. We're not even going downhill, but the powder was

so thick that it was like going through cement. One of my buddies was skiing ahead of me, and I saw him catch an edge of his
ski and fall over. Just as I was thinking, "Whoa, that's crazy!" I
caught an edge, and I fell over.

What ended up happening to me, however, was my foot got
caught and started to torque backwards. Usually, your boot will
just pop out of the ski to keep anything from breaking. Yeah,
that didn't happen with me, Mr. Advanced. My bindings weren't
going to give way at all, so one of two things was going to give
way: Either the ski was going to break or my leg was going to
break. Which one do you think broke? Yeah, I broke my tibia. I
heard it make a horrible cracking noise, and I thought, "Oh my
god. This is not good."

So, I'm lying there waiting for the ski patrol, and just my
luck, I get the new ski patroller. She's very cool, she's very nice,
but she's having a hard time figuring out how to get me on the
stretcher and take me down to the bottom of the ski hill. I don't
have a whole lot of confidence that this was going to go well. So
after about 30 minutes, I finally get in this stretcher contraption.
My buddies are kind of concerned, but I'm making light of it—
so they are *laughing like crazy* because they're great buddies.
We're even taking pictures.

As we start to go down the hill, the pain is really setting
in—it is becoming excruciating. All the blood is going to that
fracture. I know have to do something to keep my mind off
the pain and stay in good spirits. I didn't know then about how
oxytocin and dopamine really worked. I just knew that if I
concentrated on something good that I would feel better. I said
to myself, "Let's try it out. This is the perfect time, right?"

So, I started to look around me and take in the scenery with all the trees and the clouds and the sky. And I started thinking to myself, "This is beautiful; this is nature." I let myself begin to feel gratitude. In spite of my injury, I let myself feel gratitude for being out in nature, skiing, and enjoying the day with my friends. Then I let myself feel grateful for the new ski patroller who is helping me. I let all these positive emotions flood my thoughts, and—I kid you not—the pain went away. I couldn't believe it; I shocked even myself. I willed myself to keep doing it. I will myself to keep feeling gratitude and positivity. It was only later that I found out, after talking with someone about this, that a person's brain pumps out its own morphine—the oxytocin and dopamine. I was controlling that chemical release with my brain. It works. Don't take my word for it. Try it yourself. All these different tools I'm giving you have worked for me, they've worked for my clients, and they've worked for some of the best companies in the world. You have to try it for yourself. This story has a happy ending. I healed up great, and I'm even back skiing again—though now I know I'm just an intermediate skier.

More importantly, this story is also meant to get you thinking about your mood and how your mood affects you. When you go to work every day, what kind of mood are in? Think about that for a minute, because in the next section, I'm going to give you some tools to make sure that you show up to work with a positive attitude.

✳ ✳ ✳

In this section, we're going to look at the five easiest and fastest ways to control your attitude and emotions.

*1. Start every morning with a positive ritual.*

Everyone has a morning ritual. Get out of bed, brush your teeth, check your email, read the news—whatever it is for you. These rituals can affect your mood for the rest of the day. At the end of your morning ritual, how do you feel? What's your attitude? For example, if you're reading the news or you're on social media reading about whatever is going on with the world today, sometimes that news isn't always happy. Maybe you go to the gym or go for a walk right after you get up. What's your attitude like after that? Maybe, when you're in the car on your way to work, you listen to training material or positive music. I believe that a morning ritual should include an activity that energizes your mind—whether it is going into thoughts of gratitude or prayer or meditation—just some sort of spiritual activity, whatever that is for you. It will put you in a positive state of mind first thing in the morning, and this will really impact how you interact with your customers once you begin your work day. You need to have a ritual, and we'll delve into that.

*2. Move your body in the morning before work.*

You could go to the gym, or you could walk around the block, or run, or dance—anything to get the endorphins flowing through your body. Endorphins give you energy and, most importantly, your positive mood. Experts have been doing studies for years that show how activity like this can help you become up to 15 percent more productive during your work day. Always consult with your doctor about what suits you and your health level before going ahead with something like this, but try to move your body before work.

A lot of people tell me, "David, I'm just not a morning person. I like to work out in the evenings or after work." That's fine. A buddy of mine works out at lunchtime; he's been doing that forever, and that works for him. Go ahead and keep your routine, but add something in the morning to get that energy flowing. Or maybe you could try changing it up a little bit once in a while—whatever works for you. One of the main complaints I hear is, "David, I don't want to go to the gym in the morning because I need to catch up on my sleep." I know sleep is important—trust me on that. But here's the thing: If you got up even an hour earlier to go to the gym, you'll have more energy than you would if you had an extra hour of sleep. I know it sounds crazy and counterintuitive, but getting those endorphins is important. Don't take my word for it. Try it for yourself and see what happens. You're going to love the results.

*3. Eat a healthy and nutritious breakfast.*

I don't mean a coffee or a donut—a *healthy* breakfast. Like I said before, these kinds of rituals can help you become 15 percent more productive at work and have a huge impact on you throughout the day. You'll be in a better mood, you'll have more energy, and a better chance of delivering a world-class experience for your customers. Because when you're in better shape, your service is better. When your service is better, your customers notice it.

*4. Listen to positive music before work.*

Music is great. Experts have done hundreds of studies that show music affects your nervous system. We've all experienced this: You're driving along, and all of a sudden your favorite song comes on the radio. You turn it up, you get excited, and then you're dancing along to the beat. How long does it take for you to hear that song and start feeling good? It is almost instantaneous, isn't it? So, make a positive, upbeat play list for your home, for the car, for the office—to listen to before you interact with clients. You will often see professional athletes wearing headphones. They're listening to their music, getting themselves pumped up, getting themselves in the zone. They're getting into high-performance mode, and they know that music will get them in that positive mood.

Not a big music fan? Try listening training materials (maybe a few of mine, in fact). Why not play them in the car and listen all the way to work. Remember, the music and the positivity goes straight to your nervous system and will immediately affect how you feel.

*5. Use Neuro Linguistic Program (NLP) techniques.*

When I learned NLP, it was awesome. It stands for Neuro Linguistic Program. It was invented by a couple of academics who studied different psychological and psychiatric methods of self-awareness to see what worked and which would get the fastest results. And they came up with Nero Linguistic Program, NLP for short. I strongly encourage you to learn about the experts who created NLP, and there is a ton of valuable information about it on the Internet, because the techniques can really help you take control of your mindset. That's what it is about. I'm going to teach you an NLP technique that will help you literally rewire your brain.

First, stand up and take a deep breath—in through your nose, out through your mouth. Put a smile on your face (and if people are watching, tell them that you're doing this for the greater good). Take another deep breath—in through your nose, out through your mouth—and smile. Do you feel better now than you did 10 seconds ago? I bet you do. You can do this while you're driving, too. Sit up straight in your car seat, take a deep breath in, then breathe out, and then smile. Next, choose an emotion that you want to feel. Picture a moment in your life—it could have been a minute ago or earlier in your life—a moment when you felt truly happy; when, out of a possible 10 on the happiness scale, you were at an 11. Go there in your mind (and if you're doing this while driving, don't close your eyes). What did you see? What did you feel? What did you hear? Engage your senses and experience this moment as if you were there. Make your vision really bright, and put some color in it so that the color is almost popping out of the vision.

Focus on that moment and say whatever positive statements you say when you're happy. You will instantly feel that emotion because your brain can't tell whether it is really happening or not. Your brain doesn't know if it is a memory or visualization (which is what we are doing right now). When you put yourself in a positive mood, it is easier for you to accommodate and communicate with your customers. It will help you focus on positive solutions, and that's the goal. Read through this section again, really get it in your bones—and keep trying it.

Let's recap. These are the five different ways to control your attitude and emotion:

Start every morning with a positive ritual—gratitude, prayer, meditation—to put you in a positive state of mind.

Move your body, whether you're walking, running, going to the gym, dancing, or swimming. Make sure you consult a doctor so you can do what's right for your body and level of health.

Eat a healthy and nutritious breakfast. Consult a nutritionist if you need to, but make sure you're getting the energy and protein you need to get you started.

Listen to positive music on your way to work. A positive, upbeat play list is important. You don't want to dredge up bad memories with sad songs. Upbeat music. Positive music. Every day.

Use NLP techniques to rewire your brain and get rid of old habits. The most important word in business and in life is consistency. I want everyone reading this book to try this technique and all these rituals every day so that your brain makes it automatic.

If you truly want control over your attitude and your emotions, here's what *not* to do:

Don't start your day by reacting to email. Emails will only suck you down a rabbit hole for the rest of the day. Don't start your day by reacting to something negative.

Don't start your day by filling your head with negative news from the media. During my talks to audiences around the country, I challenge them to try coming out of the news for seven days. I can hear your head exploding right now. Why would I even suggest such a crazy thing? Well, most of the news is negative because that's what attracts people to it, and negativity impacts your mood.

You might think, "But I have to know what's going on. I've

got my stocks, I've got the weather, I have all these different things I need to know." I get it. If something big happens within that seven days, you'll hear about it. Trust me, someone will tell you, and you can catch up appropriately when that happens. If you absolutely must stay connected, there are apps that can help. I have an app on my phone that I use to check my stats, my stocks—I even have an app for the weather. It helps me stay in control of my time. When you watch or read the news on the Internet, you're not in control. Consider using an app that just gives you the headlines of the day.

Don't start your day listening to sad or negative music, and don't skip a nutritious breakfast. Good food gets you going for the rest of the day.

Don't focus 100 percent on a problem because it can consume your energy. Instead, try focusing 80 percent of your brain power on the solution and only 20 percent on the problem itself. You want to understand the problem, you want to understand the consequences, and the time frames, etc. But putting your energy toward the solution is the only thing that gets a result.

You guys want the ninja secret? To control your emotions and attitudes, you have to do everything we have talked about. Do them all in a way that work best for you, and do them consistently. What's the word again? Consistency. Discipline yourself. People hate that word, but discipline is the only thing that will help you enforce new habits. It can take a while to break old negative habits, especially ones you have had for 10, 20, 30 years or more. If you have a pattern of going into a defensive and aggressive state of mind when somebody's yelling at you, then you will have little chance of breaking that habit when you're trying to service an angry customer. You need to change your habits through repetition. That's the only way to do it. There's no magic; you just have to keep at it. It is not hard. In fact, it is very simple. You just need to do it.

Not only will it elevate your customer service dramatically, it will change your life forever. Imagine for a moment how your life would be with new habits and positive momentum. You'd have more energy, and you'd be happier. Isn't that worth it? Of course it is!

That was a lot of information, but we're building this foundation so that you can deliver world-class service!

✳ ✳ ✳

In this section, we are going to talk about something so important, it could not only change your business and your customer service, but it could change your life.

It is positive communication. What is positive communication? It's communicating effectively with others in such a way that it moves them toward their goal and their happiness.

The corporate world has a lot of policies and procedures that protect businesses and their customers. If you have kids or are around kids—you know this—your job is to protect them, so you say no to them to keep them from harm or even disappointment. But adults hear the word no a lot, too. We hear no so much, we often think, "Why won't somebody just say yes?"

> **A customer is four times more likely to buy from a competitor if the problem is service related versus price or product related.**

Positive communication moves people forward. In my talks, I tell audiences how to avoid the word "no." It is hard to do, but I'll give you the ninja secret. And this is my favorite one. Instead of saying no, say, "Well, I wish I could. But what I can do is…" Why is that statement so powerful? Because I kept it positive! This is what I *can* do for you. The policies and procedures are not going to change from phone call to phone call, and it's also dependent on your empowerment within your company's policies and procedures, etc. Telling a client what you can do may or may not appease them, but you are showing them that you care and that you're working to solve their problem. You're showing them what this book has been focusing on: that they're heard, that they're understood, and that they are cared for. As long as you're doing those things, you are delivering world-class customer service whether or not you can deliver whatever it is they actually want or need.

I'll give you an example. As I mentioned, I am invited to do lot of speaking engagements. Companies hire me to travel to their offices and talk about customer service. I've been doing this for several years. Earlier in my career, unfortunately, I got burned a couple of times. I do live events, and there is a lot of energy that goes into putting these together for the company, the event planner, etc. When it comes to getting paid, I set up a payment schedule that requires a deposit and then schedule to pay the remainder—or net—after the talk is delivered. I noticed that I would get my deposit sure enough, but the remainder was harder to come by. They would say, "Oh, we were going net 30 or net 60 or net 90," which means sometimes I get paid the remainder in 30 days or 60 days or even 90 days after I said goodbye to this client. Sometimes, people honestly forgot to pay the net, while others were unscrupulous and didn't pay me at all. Recently, a company hired me to speak for them. I changed my policy—and I've been using it for years now. The client agrees to pay a 50 percent deposit to book me, and then pays 50 percent seven days before the event. This way, I get paid in full, and if I can't make it for any reason—which has never happened—the company gets its money back. Very simple. This one particular client said, "We will net at 60." Clearly, this client wanted to stretch his money. So, I replied, "I wish I could do that. But what I can do for you…" I continued, "…You can pay your 50 percent deposit now and then just give me a check when I arrive." The client was happy with this. I didn't say, "NO! That's my policy or you would rip me off!" Instead, I gave them an alternative that worked out for both of us. I want you to think about how to keep transactions positive, and be mindful of the various forms of communication.

There are two types of communication: verbal and non-verbal.

*Verbal communication.* These are the words you use. This is what you said, the tone you used, and even the pace of your speaking. Here's a question for you: What do you think is more influential or more important, the words you use or the tone? What would you guess? If you guessed tone, you are correct. Sixty-five percent of your communication is based on your tone and not the words you say. I'll give you an example: You go to the grocery store, there are a million people checking out. You finally get up to the cash register, and the checker doesn't even look at you but says flatly, "Thank you for choosing our store. Can I get you bags or give you some help today?" The words were right, but did they make you feel warm and fuzzy inside? Absolutely not. If I were to say to you "Hey, I love you!" or "I love you" or "Mmmm, I love you"—they're the same words but completely different meaning depending on the tone I use. The cadences and inflections in your voice are so important. This is especially important if you're working at a call center and you're required to read a script. Make sure you're putting your mark on that script, that you're putting your emotions into it so you don't sound like a monotone robot. Good verbal communication is essential.

> ### For every customer who bothers to complain, 26 other customers remain silent.

The other type of communication is *nonverbal communication*—your facial expressions, body language, and appearance. There are 80 muscles in your face, and each one can convey a message to your clients whether you know it or not. What is your body language saying? It is telling customers whether or not you are an open person or a closed person. Your appearance has a huge impact on customer service—how you dress and your hygiene. Are you dirty and disheveled? Does your hair look like Einstein's? All of these things must be taken into account, because when somebody talks to you or they see you in person, they will judge you within the first seven seconds.

Seven seconds, that's it! You have got to get that immediate impression right—whatever it is for you.

I'll give you an example. As I've mentioned, I travel a lot for work. I'm part of a hotel rewards program, and I chose a particular hotel this one trip because its customer service is typically very high—typically! On this particular trip, I'd been flying all day, and I was super tired. When I come to this hotel, I'm used to being greeted by the hotel employees at the front desk who are usually really great. But this employee barely looked at me. She was texting (that's my pet peeve). When she finally looked up, she gives me one of those "ugh, now I've got to work" looks and proceeds to give me an uninspired welcome speech. I give her my check-in information, and she says unenthusiastically, "OK, Mr. Brownlee, thanks for being a platinum member. You get something free from our store." From her audible sighs to her body language and other nonverbal cues, she didn't make me feel like a platinum member—not at all! You have to think about all of these things together.

✶ ✶ ✶

We have reached the end of Chapter 3. We have spent this chapter giving you a foundation in the psychology behind customer service. So, let's recap. Psychology is the mental or behavioral characteristics of an individual or a group. We have to look at the psychology of our company, of our customers and, most importantly, the psychology of *you*. What can you do?

Start every morning with a positive ritual. Move your body in the morning before work. Eat a healthy and nutritious breakfast. Listen to positive music or training before work. Use NLP techniques to rewire your brain and get rid of old habits that no longer serve you well. Be sure to master positive communication—verbal and nonverbal.

Before moving on to Chapter 4, consider these few questions.

What are three core values that are most important to you? You want to make sure that these values are clear in your mind.

What are the three core values you would like to see in your company's customer service? They might be the same three or a different three, maybe in a different market.

What is your personal mission? Put another way, what would you like people to say about your accomplishments when you're gone? As a coach, I ask this of my clients, and the answer is usually "I don't really know what my personal mission is." That's OK! The great news is that it could be anything. For me, my mission is to help a million business owners and individuals find success. I want people to say that David Brownlee stood for kindness and caring, and that he helped push out that message to everyone he met. He touched lives. What is it for you?

What are the three ways you create a positive raving fan culture in the workplace? These might come from what you've learned in this book, or maybe they're ideas you're already implementing. I want you to write them down so you can think about your industry, your clients, your customers, and the people you work with—your internal clients. What are three ways you create a positive raving fan culture in the workplace? If you don't know, don't worry. I have tips in the upcoming sections that will help you.

What are three ways you could hold your teammates, your co-workers, and your leadership accountable to your core values, your mission, and your customer service goals? Because having a mission or having values is great, but if you don't hold yourself accountable to that standard, it won't matter. We've talked about those examples. So, make sure you put something in place that holds everyone accountable.

*"Open, honest communication is the best foundation for any relationship, but remember that at the end of the day it's not what you say or what you do, but how you make people feel that matters the most."*

—TONY HSIEH

*"You never get a second chance to make a first impression."*

—WILL ROGERS, STAGE AND MOTION PICTURE ACTOR, VAUDEVILLE PERFORMER

# 4

# MASTER UNDERSTANDING

I n this chapter, we're going to dive into Secret No. 4: How you understand your customers. Have you ever been in a situation where the customer comes in, has a big request, and you're struggling to understand what it is they want or how it is that you can best serve them? Do you ever have a hard time understanding your customers' or your clients' special requests—especially when they are upset or have a complicated order?

> **79% of high-income households avoid vendors for two-plus years after a bad customer experience.**

In order to make sure you understand what they want and that they understand how you can help them, here are three skills you need to learn.

*1. Ask intelligent questions.*

Ask questions in a professional manner in order to gain important information from the customers so you can better serve them. What I do with all my customers when I am talking to them over the phone is ask them tons of questions. Do you remember the 80/20 scenario we discussed in earlier chapters? This is where it applies. I am talking to them 20 percent of the time and listening to them the other 80 percent—because I want to get all the information I can in order to know how to best serve them. And I write it down. Whatever they ask me, I will respond with more questions. For example, I'll ask the people I'm training, "What's most important to you when it comes to training your team in customer service?" Then I write their answer down and say "OK, great! What else?" And I keep writing it all down. And here's an interesting secret: I write down what they tell me in the order in which they told me.

Why?

Because their brain is operating in that order, they are telling you what is most important to them. The first thing is most important, the second thing is the next most important, and so on. For good customer service, the questions should start with your greeting. I will talk about the six pillars to a world-class greeting in the next section.

Examples of using questions during your greeting include:

"Thank you for choosing my customer service. My name is David. What's your name?"

"Hi, Jennifer. How can I help you today so I can take excellent care of you?"

"Can you please tell me what happened?" Or if you're speaking to an angry customer ask, "How can I make this right for you?" "What can I do to fix this for you?"

I know those are scary questions to ask your customer, but we'll conquer that fear in this book.

*Number 2. Listen intently.*

Listen to exactly what the customer wants, and take notes as necessary. Active listening is key. Listen to what the customer says, and don't get caught up thinking about what your response is going to be.

*3. Pick up on verbal and nonverbal cues.*

In the coming chapters, we're going to take a deeper dive into what these are so you can develop a strategy that lets you provide world-class customer service.

✱ ✱ ✱

> ## Employees only ask for the customer's name 21% of the time.

In this section, we're going to look at the six pillars of a world-class greeting. Why are greetings important? Because the greeting sets the tone for the entire interaction with a client! If you don't have a professional greeting, a transaction can go downhill quickly. A professional greeting can launch a customer service transaction through the roof.

Before we dig in, I'll give you an example of a terrible service greeting: I was doing customer service training for a water company. This company delivers purified water right to your home or business. I was doing a shop-around to their competitors to see what their call centers were like. I called one particular competitor—a big international brand, and I got a voice prompt that started with the name of the company, but it wasn't the name of the brand I'd come to know. I didn't even know if I'd dialed the right number—and it was a robot voice.

The robot voice tried to get me to put in some information by dialing different numbers. After I did that, I finally got a live person who actually sounded exactly like a robot. All she said after the prompt was "ZIP code." That was the greeting—"ZIP code!" So, I gave her my ZIP code, and she just went through the motions—just like a robot. It was absolutely horrible, and I was shocked that this was the level of service from a big international brand.

So, here are the six pillars of a world-class greeting:

*1. Smile.*

Yes, smile—especially on the phone. Believe it or not, a person can tell if you're smiling even if they can't see you. If I'm smiling, you can hear it. When you aren't face to face, start that conversation with a smile. If you get an angry customer on the line, they are going to want to slap that smile right off your face. Don't let that deter you. Always start your transaction with a smile.

*2. Thank the customer.*

You must have a thankful mindset and say thank you to your customers every day. Doesn't it feel good when someone says thank you *to you*? In fact, I'll start: Thank you from the bottom of my heart for reading my book and allowing me to be your customer service coach. And if you mean it as sincerely as I do, your customer will pick up on that. It's human social interaction, and people appreciate it.

*3. Clearly state the name of the company so customers know they've reached the right place*

Have you ever called a business, and they just say hello? Sometimes, you don't know if you've reached the right number. Say the name of your company clearly and that you've reached its customer service line or department. Even if your customer walks into your business, you should still say, "Hi! Welcome to the customer service department. How can I help you today?"

*4. Introduce yourself.*

Tell them your name. Why? Because this is the beginning of the relationship. Whether this person is a regular customer who you'll meet again or a person you might meet only once for five minutes, this is your chance to develop a raving loyal client. It's the start of a relationship, and in social relationships, we use our names.

*5. Use your customer's name.*

Many studies suggest that there is no other word in any language that anyone wants to hear more than their own name, so use your customer's name throughout the transaction but especially after the initial greeting.

*6. Ask the right questions at the beginning.*

Remember to ask a question that will give you the information you need to best service your customer. Here's an example: "Hi, thank you for choosing Pure Customer Service. My name is David. What's your name? Jennifer? Nice to meet you, Jennifer. How can I help you today?" If there's a problem or request, ask for specifics—and write it all down.

All of these pillars combined might have you thinking, "This sounds like a script, and I hate scripts. They're inauthentic. It just makes me sound like a robot." I get it, but you can take these suggestions and make them your own. You can tweak them to make them feel right and comfortable for you. Why are scripts important? Consistency is important in customer service. You want to answer the phone the same way for every customer and every transaction to make sure you deliver that world-class customer service to new customers as well as returning customers. It doesn't matter whether you work in a big call center or retail store—you want that consistency.

If you eat at an international hamburger chain and you order a hamburger—whether you get one in the states or you get one in Europe—it's should be same quality, right? Customer service is the same. That consistent quality helps build your brand and attract clients. Think of the biggest brand names that you know and love because of the luxury or service or price they provide. You expect that brand to deliver at a certain level—that's what consistency is all about. You want everybody on the same page in your chain. So, customize a script, give it your own flavor, and own it every time—whether it's on a phone call, email, live chat, text, or in person. Make sure you've got that consistency.

So, let's recap the six pillars of a world-class greeting:

1. Smile.
2. Thank the customer.
3. State the name of the company clearly to make sure they know they've reached the right place.
4. Introduce yourself and use your name because you're building a relationship.
5. Use the customer's name—because they want to hear it. It's also part of relationship building.

6. Ask intelligent questions to get the information you need so you can best serve them—and write it all down.

> ## Hi! Thank you for choosing Pure Customer Service. My name is David. What's your name? Nice to meet you, Jennifer. How can I help you today?

What happens next? In this section, we're going to talk about a skill that is incredibly important in customer service. It's called listening intently. Not just listening but *listening intently*. There are two types of listening that we'll cover in this section: active listening and passive listening.

The first type of listening we'll cover is called active listening—and this is what we *want* you to do. It is important that you make eye contact with the customer, that you're processing and acknowledging what the customer is saying, that you're engaged with and showing compassion for your customer. You want to give personalized responses to the customer. You must listen to exactly what the customer wants and not what you want. And you should be taking notes if that's a process that works for you. It's also important to acknowledge verbally that you're listening to the customer, so you might occasionally say things like "yes," "absolutely," "of course." That way, they know they're being heard—and that's what your customers want. They want to know that they're being heard and being understood. And in order to be heard and understood, you have to actively listen to them.

The second type of listening is passive listening. Here's how I describe it: Passive listening is when you're gazing elsewhere when somebody is talking to you. Has anyone ever done that to you? Of course. We all do that. Sometimes we get distracted—we're just somewhere else. Maybe you are passively listening because you're formulating your response while the customer is talking. Maybe it happens in a social setting, like when you're at a party and someone is telling you a great story, and while they're telling you, you are thinking of a similar story. You might be thinking—while they're talking—"Oh my god! I can't wait for them to finish their story so I can tell them my story." That's happened to you, right? You probably know someone like that. It's definitely something that happens to me.

And sometimes it could be that you're just thinking about something else while someone is talking to you; you're just *not there* and end up assuming what your customer is saying. In customer service, we get so many phone calls and so many customers who come in. We think we've heard it all, don't we? A person calls with a problem or question, and we think we already know where the transaction going. And what happens is that your brain shuts off, and you stop listening. It's usually at times like this that the transaction goes in a completely different direction than what we expected. That is why, as customer service professionals, we have to make sure we're always *actively* listening.

Another aspect of passive listening is the generalized response—a scripted response. A lot of companies use what's called decision trees. This is particularly true in call centers. Basically, a decision tree dictates that when a customer says this, you say that. They ask this, and you answer that. We've all been on the customer side of a call like this. I have. I'm sure you have, too. We know it doesn't personalize the experience at all. I'm sure you've thought, "Is this person even listening to me?" The client doesn't feel heard or understood, and that means the transaction is not going down the right track.

I'll give you an example. I mentioned in the introduction that I also own an entertainment/production company. We provide all kinds of entertainment for special events from DJs and bands to lighting, sound and video production. We do this all in a live setting, so we will even provide catering and security. You name it, we do it. We are in L.A., so a lot of our clients have been major Hollywood movie studios. One year, we were privileged enough to be able to provide the DJ services for a major Hollywood studio that was throwing a big Academy Awards after-party. All the celebrities, paparazzi, and everyone you can think of would be there. We had a pre-meeting with the client at which my partner (at the time) and I were both listening when the client said: "There's this one '70s disco song that we *do not* want played. Here's the song. Don't play it," We understood. It was an easy request. Out of all the millions of songs that could be played, there was only one song they didn't want to hear— super easy. So, the night of the red carpet event arrives, and there are limousines, paparazzi, and camera flashes going off from every direction. It was absolutely amazing. Everything was going great. I'm downstairs, the DJ is up in the booth, and people are out on the dance floor. To set the scene, I'm pretty far away from the DJ at this point when all of a sudden I hear that one disco song that the client expressly asked us not to play.

Everything stopped—like a record scratch. It was like every-thing after moment happened in slow motion. I see people with walkie-talkies communicating with each other, and I'm think-ing "Oh my god! No! This is horrible!" Then I feel the client grab me by the shoulder and pull me around, and this person says, "What's going on?" I say, "I don't know." The client was understandably furious.

This is why listening intently is so important. I did get this client back many years later—and it was the same team of people that was there that night, so they all remembered what happened. It took many years to win back their trust. Lesson learned: Listen intently and use active listening, really be in the conversation—because we want to make them feel understood and heard, and we also want them to feel cared for.

✳ ✳ ✳

In this section, we're going to talk about how to build rap-port with a limited amount of time. So, what's rapport? It's the foundation of a relationship. We build rapport every day with the people that we meet. It's about finding that commonality and familiarity that makes us feel comfortable with each other. And it's very important in customer service, especially world-class customer service, that our clients and our customers feel comfortable with us. There are four ways to do this.

*1. Talk about general topics.*

Use small talk, like the weather, the local sports team, and, of course, news events. I'm telling you not to watch the news too much, but if there's something big going on, then it's a good way to get a conversation going.

*2. Make a specific observation.*

For example, clothing; if someone is wearing a sweatshirt from UCLA, you could say, "My sister went to UCLA"; or jewelry, "I like your necklace." It only takes half a second to do, but it's big.

*3. Avoid talking about politics and religion.*

Those kinds of conversations can backfire really fast.

*4. Always acknowledge the customer—especially if they're waiting.*

If you're in retail, and there's a long line to make a purchase, just quickly acknowledge the next customer by holding up your finger and saying, "Hey, I'll be right with you." If you're on the phone and have people waiting in the queue or on hold, and a client call is taking a long time, come back on the line and say, "I apologize for the wait. Would you like me to call you back? I honor your time." People really appreciate that as you make them feel cared for.

These are the basics. But we're going to go deeper. Let's dive in to how to build rapport.

> It is 6 to 7 times more expensive to acquire a new customer than it is to keep a current one.

*Matching and Mirroring.*

We're going to discuss matching and mirroring. Have you heard this term? Matching and mirroring is an instinctive way that people build relationships with other people. Matching and mirroring is picking up on bodily cues or what a person is saying. We'll discuss exactly how to do that in a bit, but let's talk a bit more about what it is. Matching and mirroring usually happens naturally. Sometimes we don't even realize it because it happens at a subconscious level. The next time you're at a party, take a look around the room and see how people like to sit. Some people sit with their legs crossed, some sit with their legs apart. You'll notice that when people have been sitting close together for a while, the pairs or groups of people will begin to cross their legs the same way or set their arms the same way—maybe folded or hanging at their sides, for example.

Why does this happen? It's called entrainment, and it's a natural brain process that makes people feel comfortable around other people. This happens in nature, and it is one of those brilliant things that humans and animals and objects do that is instinctive and hard to explain. It's like a clockmaker who has hundreds beautiful grandfather clocks in his studio. When you walk into that studio, given enough time, all the pendulums will begin to swing together—without anything forcing them to do so. It just occurs naturally. Entrainment happens among groups of women who live together. Their menstrual cycles will begin to sync up. That's entrainment.

But matching and mirroring is something you can also do intentionally to more quickly build a common bond in a relationship. What kinds of things are we talking about? The first thing is body language. You can actually match and mirror a person's body language. For example, if somebody is sitting with their arms crossed, you can also cross your arms while you're talking to them. You don't want to mimic them, but if they cross their legs next, you can cross yours similarly in a casual way during your conversation. They're not going to notice it consciously, but it will subconsciously make them feel a connection with you. This is ninja stuff, and it goes without saying that you should only use this tool for the forces of good. Repeat after me: forces of good. This tool is to be used to influence someone so you can take care of that person in the best way possible. I want to really make sure that you use all these tools for the good of your customers but internal and external.

*Breathing.*

Do this especially when you're on the phone. If you notice someone is breathing in a rhythm, you can pick up on the same rhythm as that person. Again, their subconscious is going to pick up on it, and it will make them feel more comfortable.

*Volume.*

This is especially good for phone work, but it applies to all transactions. If somebody is speaking loudly during a phone conversation, but you're answering them quietly, what will that make them think of you? They might think, "This person doesn't care! They're not as excited as I am." On the flip side, if somebody is speaking quietly or timidly, and you are being overly enthusiastic, that person might think you're trying to pull something over on him or her. I know that I'm a loud and enthusiastic speaker—that's part of what I do for a living. But I learned that, for some jobs and for some people, I had to tone it down a little bit.

*Cadence.*

Cadence is how fast you're speaking. In different parts of the country, people talk at different speeds. Take some-body from New York, for example. Do they speak slowly or quickly? Generally, they speak quickly, right? You have that fast-talking client from New York. But what if you're down

South? How do they speak in the South? Faster or slower? They speak a little slower down there. So, you've got to match and mirror your cadence to make a customer in any part of the country feel more comfortable.

This is a lot of information, but try it out for yourselves. Go to a bar or a restaurant. If you're sitting or eating, this works perfectly. Pick a person in the restaurant who is about 10 or 15 feet away from you—but they can't be looking at you directly. You should be in their peripheral vision. Now, when that person goes to take a drink, you take a sip of your drink. When they cross their legs, you cross your legs. If they go to buy their food, you go to buy your food. Try this for about 10 or 15 minutes. They'll pick up on you doing this, though it will be subconsciously. If you're doing it right, they won't think you're mimicking them. All they're going to think is, "Gosh, do I know that person? Wow, I wonder who that person is." If you're single, this is a great tip for meeting people. You can do it anywhere. It even works at a library. Don't take my word for it. Go out and try it for yourself. It will blow you away.

To recap: Building rapport by using matching and mirroring is something people do naturally; it's entrainment. And you do this via your body language, breathing rhythm, voice volume and cadence. In the customer service field, you can build rapport more quickly by doing it intentionally to better satisfy your client. It's about building that common bond and relationship, because that's what this is all about—connections.

How do we do this for internal customers? That's coming up in the next section.

★ ★ ★

> **7 in 10 Americans say they are willing to spend more money with companies that they believe provide excellent customer service.**

We're going to continue talking about how to build rapport in this section—but for the workplace with your internal customers. These are your employees, your leadership team, and people who you see every day at work. How do you build rapport with them? This will build on everything we've learned so far, like matching and mirroring, entrainment, and observation—all these things apply to your internal customers, too. For the workplace, we want to talk about the importance of the "morning huddle." These huddles can be held afternoon or evening, too, but the main idea is to gather your team together before they start their shift, almost like a pre-shift meeting with a little something extra. In this section, I'm going teach you exactly how to do it and what makes a successful huddle.

There are five stages to a world-class huddle, and it only takes about five to 10 minutes. Here, too, the key is consistency. You must do these huddles regularly. They have an amazing effect on morale and on productivity, and they are a great way to build rapport with your team that helps create a positive attitude among them every day. The foundation of customer service, especially world-class customer service, is you. It all starts with a leader's positive attitude with their frontline people. These frontline people need to be feeling energized, and a pre-shift huddle is a great way to do that. There are five terrific things you can do in a huddle that will make them productive and positive.

*1. Share a positive quote.*

I love this one. It could be from anybody. It could be from one of the leadership members in your organization, it could be from a poet or a musician, even from an ancient Chinese text. It could be anything as long as it's something uplifting, something that creates a positive change in your body, and gives you a positive attitude. Even the act of reading out your company's core values—whatever they are and however many you have—can inspire your team. I would read through those core values to really get them in your head and into your team members' heads. If I were to ask you right now what are your core values? Do you know? Maybe you know them, maybe you don't. The huddle is a great way to get them ingrained among your staff. You could also regularly read out the company mission statement together as a team. Consider adding music to the huddle—to increase the positive effect. This part of the huddle process shouldn't take more than one to two minutes.

*2. Share a positive testimonial.*

Has a customer or employee or reviewer said something good about your company or representatives, or about your product or service? Take that positive testimonial and share it with your team. It's going to help build morale, create a deeper relationship with the company, and promote teamwork. Discuss the testimonial in your huddle for about one to two minutes.

*3. Discuss which best practice led to the positive testimonial and then record and measure what's working.*

This will help you and your team start building that world-class customer service consistency. We're taking what works—the best practices—and making sure everyone knows them and knows they apply to everyone. Do you see where we're going with this? Are you starting to connect the dots? Now we're starting to up our game, creating A-players by capitalizing on the things that work. Also, even though we do most of these actions intentionally, it's also great to recognize and acknowledge when something unintentional works—and also share that with the team during the huddle.

*4. Challenges and solutions.*

You are always going to come across challenges. What I hear time and time again is that the customer service reps and the teams don't feel heard or understood or cared for by the management. A huddle gives them an open forum to do some controlled venting. Managers should let employees vent a little bit and let them come to them with the challenges they're facing. In a huddle, the group as a whole can respond: "Hey! That happened to me once, and here's what I did to overcome that challenge." Leadership can learn from these huddles ways tell employees during future interactions, for example, "Well, this is what you do in this situation. This is how you turn it around." Whatever the challenge is—meeting deadlines, dealing with angry customers—during a huddle someone gets to share their challenges, and the group or manager can offer solutions.

*5. State change.*

This is huge because the state of your attitude and how you feel will directly impact the level of service your customers get out of you and your team. Have you ever been so embarrassed by something you did that you can't believe you even did it, while at other times, you felt so good about what you did that you owned it and said, "Hah! Yes, I did that." It depends on how you feel in that given moment. When you're feeling good, are you more likely to perform better? Yes! Absolutely. And this can impact the team! It's like playing football: You get into that huddle before or after or during the game, and the players pump themselves up, even if they're in a funk. Your team, in these huddles, should do some deep breathing and stretching. Take all that in, give each other high fives, use a mantra that you guys have, or give each other hugs—whatever works for you. Just make sure it's something to get people pumped up before they face the clients. Boom! You have created an energy that changes attitudes.

Let's do a quick review of the morning huddle. The whole process should take five to 10 minutes before a shift starts in the morning, afternoon, or evening. First, share a positive quote. Then, share a positive testimonial to deepen the relationship among employees and their relationship to the company, and discuss what best practice led to that result so you're raising the bar for everybody. Then let the team discuss a challenge they're facing and allow everyone to contribute toward coming up with a solution. Then state change: breathe, stretch, give high-fives or hugs, or recite a team mantra to pump you up before you get ready to go out on the floor to greet customers. Now, you guys are ready to rock.

> 78% of consumers have bailed on a transaction or not made an intended purchase because of a poor service experience.

In this section, we're going to talk about how to build rapport with a client in 30 seconds or less. I came up with acronym that I want you to learn. I love acronyms! It's called S.E.C.—because it only takes a *sec* to do.

S = smile.

E = eye contact.

C = comment or compliment.

I want you to write down this acronym and its meaning, and post it on your computer or stick it on your refrigerator—because it's a big one. And always remember it before you pick up the phone or greet a customer or talk to a client. It's going to help you remind yourself to deliver that world-class customer service. Let's dive deeper into the three pillars of this acronym.

The S stands for smile. Seems so basic, right? Smile. But with everything that's happening in life, at work, especially if there are people in line or there's a lot of pressure to get stuff done quickly, we forget to smile. Just take a second and smile, reset and go. Then you greet the client. Because smiles are contagious, aren't they? Unless you are a really grumpy person, if somebody's smiling at you, your instinct is to smile back. Let me prove it to you right now. Don't take my word for it, try this exercise: Smile right now. Just smile. While you're smiling, try to make yourself upset. Get angry about something, but keep smiling. Get really upset; get really angry. You can't do it, can you? Why not? Because the physical act of smiling is sending a message to your brain that you're happy. Even if you're not happy, the message is still sent to your brain, and you will actually begin to feel happy.

Depression is a huge problem for so many people in this country. A study out of Stanford asked patients suffering from depression to smile in front of the mirror for 20 minutes every day. The study found that when they were smiling, their mood changed. Smiling seems so simple—because it is. It's very easy to do; you just have to remember to do it. Common sense isn't always common practice, is it? Sometimes, we just forget, so make sure you remember to smile. That's step one.

The E stands for eye contact. Why is that important? When you're making eye contact with a person, you're letting them know that you're paying attention, that you're ready to listen to them intently, and understand and care for them. You're showing them through action that you're engaged and present. If I'm looking you in the eye, and I suddenly look away, you will feel as though we lost that connection. So, make that eye contact. It tells your clients that you're ready to engage with them and serve them.

Lastly, C stand for comment or compliment. A little comment about the weather or about lighthearted news, or maybe a local sports team or a food you enjoy is a good conversation starter. As for compliments, you want to keep it classy, not creepy. Something like, "Hey, I like that necklace," is a perfect example of a good compliment. And, fellas, be careful with your compliments, especially with women—remember: classy, not creepy.

> 76% of consumers say they view customer service as the true test of how much a company values them.

There's a Mexican restaurant that I love. It's not really fast food, but you go in there and you pick out what you want—like a burrito or taco or salad—and they make it for you as you go down the line. This one time, a woman was standing behind me in the line, and the employee who was working on my burrito at that moment looked up at the lady and said, "You know what? I really like that shade of lipstick on you." She said this pretty loudly so everyone could hear. The woman looked at her and said, "Excuse me?" The woman behind the counter said it again. "I really like that shade of lipstick on you." You could see the lady next to me start to smile—and blush a little bit— just from one simple compliment. The employee probably made this woman's day, maybe even her week or month or year. Who knows when the last time was that she received a compliment? Just a little act of kindness or caring may have had a huge ripple effect on this person. She may go home and pass on that kindness to her kids or husband, or go to work the next day and treat her employees a little better. And you have the power to do that as a customer service professional. So just try giving a simple comment or compliment, and see what happens.

We have to remind ourselves to do things like this every day, because the question is not whether we know it or not but whether we implement it and how consistently we implement it.

Let's do a quick review. S.E.C.: S stands for smile. E stands for eye contact. C stands for comment or compliment. If you get nothing else out of this book, just remember S.E.C., and that alone will elevate your customer service to world-class, because you will have the attitude of gratitude for these clients.

✱ ✱ ✱

Next up, we're going to talk about the importance of picking up on verbal and nonverbal cues. Earlier, we talked about positive communication, and there are two ways to communicate: verbally and nonverbally.

Clients will communicate with you both verbally and nonverbally, but the statistics say that 96 percent of your unhappy customers won't even tell you they're unhappy, and 91 percent of your unhappy customers just won't come back. That's powerful. So, you need to pick up on the cues whether they're telling you directly or not. You need to be able to read their words and their actions and behaviors. When you look at a baby, sometimes he or she is just staring at you, looking at your face, looking into your eyes, your soul. They work with expressions because they can't talk. Babies are cued in to your facial expressions because your facial expressions say so much to them.

> 66% of customers switch companies due to poor service. 82% felt that their service provider could have done something to prevent them from switching.

Let's start with verbal communication. Verbal cues are all about listening and understanding what a person's response is telling you. It's about paying close attention to these factors.

*1. Tone of voice.*

If you provide a remedy or solution for somebody, and you ask them, "Is that good for you? Is that a good solution?" and they respond by saying, "Yeah, that's great" in a slow, reluctant tone, it's up to you to recognize that this customer may not be satisfied. Don't just let it go. If you can clearly tell that they're upset, and you ignore that, it could come back to bite you. Before just saying, "OK! Thanks for calling!" and hanging up, try asking the customer if there is anything else you can do or saying, "Maybe we can explore a different remedy." Believe me, if that client is not satisfied, they'll call back and complain more. Remember when we talked about how world-class customer service saves you time? If you put in the brainpower and extra time during this part of a trans-action, it will save you time later. So, listen to their tone of voice—it's very important.

*2. Pay attention to the words customers choose to express themselves.*

If you ask a customer, "Is there anything else I can do for you?" and you sense something's off, always address it. Ask them, "Hey, is there something that I've missed?" and keep that conversation going—get to the bottom of it. The client may not always be right about a situation, but the client should always leave happy and satisfied. Make that your goal; make that your mantra. If you're on the phone with a customer, and they are using angry words and sound exasperated—address it. You have to pick up on it. We're going to talk about the future of customer service later in the book—which is leaning heavily toward automation. A robot cannot pick those things up, but you can. This ability can add value to the company. You don't want to lose your job to a robot, do you? So, make sure you pick up on these verbal cues and address them. Can you appease everybody 100 percent of the time? No. But if you're appeasing people 90 percent of the time, how hard would it be to take it to 99 percent? That's only 9 percent more, and it can make a huge impact on your commission check, your paycheck, and your opportunity for advancement.

Let's move on to nonverbal cues. These are mainly facial expressions. Humans have 80 muscles in their faces alone. Going back to the baby example, babies will look at your face and decide whether someone is nice or mean. They are studying your face because your face tells a story regardless of the words that are coming out of your mouth. If you're on the phone or dealing with a customer in person, and that person is giving you the silent treatment—oh, silence can be deadly. You need to pick up on the nonverbal cues and address them. Just keep delving deeper and deeper by asking questions to figure out what the real problem is so you can address it. Negative nonverbal cues include frowning, head shaking and closed body language, such as crossed arms, sighing, and shallow breathing. These cues let you know that a customer is getting upset. It is your job as a world-class service provider to be able to recognize these nonverbal cues, and then work toward getting the customer or client to tell you the problem so you can listen and understand. Pay close attention to sighing, metaphors, body language, facial expressions, extended silence—any of those things.

The same goes for positive nonverbal cues. As we've discussed in this book, smiling comes through. You can see a smile; you can hear when someone is smiling over the phone. If you see a customer nodding his or her head—that is a positive affirmation using body language. They're telling you that you're doing something right and that you should continue doing it. Keep responding to that energy right to the end of a transaction. Look for smiling, grinning, head nodding, open body language.

✷ ✷ ✷

In this section, we're really going to look at personality management. This is one of my favorite things to teach. Why? Because customer service is very skill and personality based. You've got to know these skills, and you've got to have the right attitude because you're building a foundation. In order to get your team to use these skills consistently at a world-class level, you must be able to coach them, relate to them, and influence them. And that's what you're going to learn. I often meet with customer service managers, executives, and supervisors who say to me, "I can't just get the employees to implement the stuff we're teaching them."

This is how you do it; this is going to be great for you.

I call it C.I.S.A. I told you I love acronyms. C.I.S.A. stands for four personality types. I'll tell you what each of these means in a bit, but first let me explain the idea around the acronym. The idea is that in order to influence somebody, especially in your company, in your customer service, you must align your core values personally to that of the company and its mission. A person will be influenced the when they can attach what already influences them to what you ask them to do. I'll show what I mean by that as we go on. Now let's unpack this acronym.

C = captain

I = inspiration

S = status quo

A = analytical

The C stands for being a captain. What kind of traits does a captain have? These are the people who get things done. They're very decisive. They don't let anything stand in their way. They're like bulldozers. Maybe they are the CEOs or management. They are very successful, but they often possess negative traits that you should also be aware of. Captains can often come across as too abrasive or too aggressive or impatient. A captain may be so focused on getting things done that he or she isn't necessarily thinking about how those negative traits are impacting the people around them.

Next is I, and it stands for being an inspiration. These are the people who have a magnetic personality. You just want to follow their lead. They get along seemingly effortlessly with everybody. You just want to know what they're going to say next. And what's so great about this personality type is that are able to easily build those relationships we've talk about and influence others. They're very good at it. Is there a negative to being an inspiration? Yes. Someone who falls under this personality trait needs to be aware that when they are talking with people, many of them will be too quick to trust them and end up getting burned. How? People with this personality trait tend not to focus on the details; they're usually much better at handling the big picture stuff. They'll often leave the details to someone else, and sometimes that backfires. The captain often works in the same way.

These two personality types—the captain and the inspiration—are extroverts. They're outgoing. What's interesting about these four traits—you'll more about the other two shortly—is that we have all four of these personality types within us. You might say, "But, David, I'm an introvert." Maybe you are, but you still may have the more outgoing traits within you, just at a lower frequency. For most people, one or two of these traits really stand out clearly, but the other two are there in the background. We'll get into that in a bit, too.

S stands for being a status quo personality. What does this mean? Status quo personality types like things the way they are—that's what status quo means. These people don't like change that much, but they excel at building those deep loyal relationships within the company. Do you know anyone whose loyalty is off the charts? It can take a while to build a relationship with a person who is a status quo personality type, but once it's made, it's like super glue. These are the employees who've been doing their jobs at their companies for decades. What are their negative traits? Well, because one of their soft spots is that they don't like change, they can be slow to make decisions. Extroverts are quick to make decisions—but they may not be the right ones. Introverts want to take it slow and maintain the status quo.

Last but not least, the A stands for analytical personality types. These are people who like numbers and organization, and so they are typically accountants or librarians. These are people who love order, they are reliable and precise, and they are always striving for perfection. You can always rely on them to get the numbers right, because that's what they love to do. Like the status quo personality, they really don't like to move fast because they don't like change; they like predictability. These people are also generally introverts.

Here's a question for you: After looking at all four of the personality traits above, which one of these is the best for customer service? Here's what I'll tell you: They are all equal.

The fact is, one or more of these traits describes who you are at your core. You might be one trait but wish you could be more like another, so you try changing. But that change in your personality will not last because it goes against who you are. You won't feel in alignment with your true personality and strengths. So, here's what I tell my clients: Embrace who you are. Adapt when you need to for certain situations, but go back to being who you are and be proud of it, and use your strengths to do your best work. This is harder for some people than others. Make sure your job aligns with what you like to do, who you are, and who you want to be.

I worked with a client who said to me, "You know, we have this new customer service person, and she's just not cutting it. She's very dry, bland—she's not personable." I told the client that I would have a conversation with her. I listened in on one of her phone calls with a customer. My client was right on the nose. It was clear she was uncomfortable. I sat down with her and asked her about her background before working with this company. She said she started as an accountant—with this company. She'd been an accountant for 10 years. She was great at it, and that's what she liked doing—she liked the orders and numbers. She liked knowing what was coming because she knew how to manipulate it. That was her personality. She told me that she came to work one day, and her supervisor said that her services as an accountant were no longer needed and that she was being transferred to customer service. She freaked out but took the job anyway. She didn't know what to do, and she really didn't want to come out of her comfort zone. I knew that didn't mean she *couldn't* do it. She and I worked together to accommodate her personality into her work, and she's much better at customer service now.

When you choose a career in customer service, you know you'll be interacting with people. How does this apply to you as a customer service manager or leader? When you sit down with your people, you need to be thinking about what type of personality this person has.

If you're talking to a captain, how do you influence them? Well, don't bug them with the details. Just tell them what you want, and they'll get it done for you. That's how you influence this type of person.

With an inspiration-type personality, take a little more time. Let them tell you a story, relate to them on a social level. People in customer service are social creatures, they like talking to people and interacting with them.

With a status quo personality, slow it down a little bit. Show them how they can find stability in whatever it is you need them to do. Show them how to enjoy this stability.

When you're trying to work with someone who's analytical, pull out the spreadsheet. Take your time with them, and let them look through the data. With an analytical type, show don't tell. Show them the data that explains how to do whatever it is that you want them to do.

C.I.S.A. personality types also apply to customers. Let's say you're a customer service rep, and you're taking phone calls and helping people throughout the day. If you've got the captain, give them the solution quickly; they don't want to mess with the details. If you get an inspiration-type customer, just get ready for that longer talk time during your transaction. Ask them what they want, and take your time with them. For a status quo client, slow it down for them. Speak a little slower and softer, and show them how this steadiness works. And with an analytical customer, pull out the data.

★ ★ ★

In this chapter, you learned about asking intelligent questions and gathering that information to best serve your customers. You also learned about what it takes to listen intently—active versus passive listening. You also learned about the six pillars of a world-class greeting. It's key! You have to set the tone for that first impression. You also learned about how to ask the right questions to really get the information that will help you best serve your customers. And you also learned how to build rapport and do it quickly, how to use matching and mirroring, and S.E.C.—smile, eye contact, comment and compliment—and also about verbal and nonverbal cues, and of course, C.I.S.A., which is all about personality management.

That is a lot to process, so here are some exercises you can do on your own to help you retain it.

1. Create a world-class greeting that you commit to using and practicing every day. You can use the ones I describe earlier in this chapter, but I encourage you to create something that's uniquely yours and implement it consistently.

2. Write down an experience you had with an angry customer and how you could have used understanding to help create a positive interaction with that person.

3. Try implementing huddles with your team before a daily shift—morning, afternoon, or evening. If you're a solo

entrepreneur, trying to have your own solo huddle and measure your results. Get yourself pumped up because you've got to have that positive attitude when you start interacting with your customers.

4.  Try a matching and mirroring challenge. This is for extra credit! This is the *real* challenge if you're willing to take it. Go to a restaurant and choose someone sitting 10 to 15 feet away from you, stay in his or her peripheral vision, not in direct view. Then match and mirror the person's behavior. When they take a sip of their drink, you do the same; when they take a bite of their food, you take a bite of your food; when they cross their legs, you cross your legs. After about 10 to 15 minutes, they'll look at you as if they know you.

Most importantly, keep practicing and enjoy yourself.

*"Don't find fault, find a remedy."*

—HENRY FORD

*"Rule number one, use your good judgment in all situations. There are no additional rules."*

—NORDSTROM EMPLOYEE HANDBOOK

# 5

# RESPONSE AND RESPONSIBILITY

> Top 2 reasons for customer loss:
> 1. Customers feel poorly treated.
> 2. Failure to solve a problem in a timely manner.

We are now at Secret No. 5—Response and Responsibility. This is a really important section that discusses a challenging aspect of customer service. Have you ever received a phone call at work from someone who is upset at you only to find out the problem had nothing to do with you? Maybe it was a co-worker or a manager, or maybe it was a shipping company you're working with—but the problem was something that was totally out of your control. How do you deal with that type of situation? That's what we're going to talk about in this section. Do your customers care if the problem is your fault or not? No. They just want to get their issue resolved, and it is your job to respond appropriately to your customer's needs and concerns, and take responsibility in that moment for your company's service, regardless of whether or not you are at fault.

Some companies take this philosophy to a whole other level. I'll give you an example. Several years ago, I was fortunate enough to go on tour with a musician. In addition to my work as a customer service coach, I also play guitar, I sing, and I rap—I do all these different things. A while back, I put a band together for a very talented female artist who had a No. 1 album in Japan. She typically plays dance tracks when she's performing, but she and her team wanted a live band to accompany her. I have been a musician for many years, and so the producer called me asking if I could put a band together. I assembled a team of all-stars: professionals, music directors, bass players, drummers, keyboard players, guitar players—everything. I made myself the rhythm guitar player, and I made myself the rapper and the hype guy. It was so much fun. I even went on tour with her to Japan! I had the best experience, and it was my first time in Japan.

This artist was with one of the big record companies, and their team spared no expense. They picked us up from the airport and took us to this amazing hotel. The next morning, before we were getting ready to leave, I needed to change some currency, and I needed to get some coffee. There was a Starbucks right next door to the hotel, where I stopped in and got a cup. When I got back to the hotel, I sat down in the lobby and put my coffee down next to me, but then I had to get up for a minute and—BOOM! My coffee went flying. It spilled all over the floor and the counter. I felt horrible; it was completely my fault. The nice lady behind the counter told me to relax. I said I wanted to clean it up, and she said no. Before I knew it, it was like something out of a movie. Two people came running out from the back. One person had a towel and asked me what I was drinking. I tell her it was a regular black coffee. Another person takes off to the Starbucks next door. The person with the towel came to me first and didn't even worry about the mess at the counter or the floor. Instead, they towel *me* off. Then somebody comes running toward me with another fresh cup of coffee from Starbucks. I couldn't believe it. The spill wasn't even their fault—it was my fault, my clumsiness.

That was world-class service.

Ask yourself what you are doing to make sure your response to a problem is appropriate. Are you taking responsibility for the problem even when it is not your fault? I know that's tough to do. But when someone calls, and they are yelling at you for something you didn't do, you need to have the tools and strategies to get through that situation.

> **26% of consumers have experienced being transferred from agent to agent and never got their problem resolved.**

In this section, we're going to look at the five keys to mastering your response to situations like this and taking responsibility. When the customer calls you, they don't care who is at fault for the problem they are experiencing. They only care about getting it resolved.

*1. Reassure your customers.*

Let your clients know that you are going to take care of them. *You.* For example, if you work at a hotel and a customer calls you at the front desk saying, "Hey, my light bulb is out," you may not be the one physically going to change that light bulb, but you are the person who is going to get that light bulb changed. *You* are going to call maintenance and get a technician to take care of it. When that customer calls you in that moment, even though it is not your fault the light is out and you are not the one who's going to fix it, you still need to reassure the guest that you are going to make sure that it gets replaced. You also want them to know you will be with them every step of the way. Tell them, "I'm going to check back in with you to make sure that it got done." Another example: Say you're working at a big-box store and a customer is looking for a particular product. It is great practice to walk the customer over to where that product is—even if you are doing something else and don't have the time. Take that extra minute or two to walk them over to where they will find what they're looking for or take them to someone who can help them if you can't.

You take responsibility in that moment. This is world-class service—and it is going to make all the difference in the world to your business. That customer is going to feel cared for. I know I'm using these phrases over and over, but it's because I really want to get them sink into your bones. *Your customers want to feel cared for.* You should *want* to put the customer at ease and let them know that you're there to serve them and take care of them. To do that, here are some examples of things you can say: "I will do whatever I can to make sure we resolve this for you"; "I'm here now, and I promise to take excellent care of you"; "I will do everything I can to make sure you leave happy." I love that last one! What you say will help a person who is struggling with a problem to control their focus. Let me give you another example. Let's say you have an angry customer. They are just—ARGH!—all over the place. You might say, "I will do everything I can to make sure you leave happy." In that moment, if they are listening to what you are saying, where does their focus go? To leaving happy. Just by saying that simple phrase, you can refocus their mindset toward a happy resolution. I am going to give you some more tools and simple phrases you can use to get them to that happy place. I will also teach you how your tone can show your sincerity. These tools will make a big difference.

*2. Respond quickly.*

You may not be able to solve a problem quickly, but you must respond quickly. Show the customer or client that their request is important by taking some action right away—send an email, make a phone call, talk to your manager. Begin working on a solution, whatever it is, so that the customer knows this is important to you. When you say, "I will take care of this for you right away!"—mean it.

*3. Respond positively.*

We talked about this earlier in the book. You want to do everything you can to avoid using the word no. Sometimes you have to use it, but if you can make it you're goal to avoiding using the word no, you are going to naturally use it a lot less often. You'll find positivity and positive communication will become a habit. My favorite one is, "I wish I could do that, but what I *can* do for you is…" I am changing a customer's focus from what I can't do to what I *can* do. "What I can do" sounds like you are working toward a solution. The subconscious is going to pick up on that. The ultimate solution you offer them instead may not be what they want, but they will remember the transaction positively.

*4. Take responsibility even if it is not your fault.*

You must be the one to apologize. It is not like you're going to be able to get the shipping guy who delivered the wrong package on the phone to apologize to your client. *You* must be the one to apologize in that moment. You should say things like:

"I apologize."

"I know how frustrating that can be."

"I am here now, and I promise to take excellent care of you."

There is not much more you can say than that, right? "I apologize" is the sincerest thing you can say. Another note about apologizing to a customer: Avoid saying "I'm sorry." I'm sorry is too general; it doesn't express culpability for whatever happened. When someone passes away or somebody's feeling bad, you say I'm sorry—because you are sympathizing with that person. An apology is different. "I apologize" is a phrase that takes ownership of a situation. You can even take it one step further. You can say, "Please forgive me." When you ask a person to forgive you, you are asking them to participate in this apology with you. It's a subtle but very important change. When you say, "Please forgive me," most people will say, "OK, I do."

BOOM! You've got them, and subconsciously they will come down a notch if they are upset.

*5. Let your customer vent.*

You've got to let them release that frustration. Let them unload on you. I know it won't feel good in that moment, but let them do it. Let them blow off that steam. We're going to look at this in more detail in a bit.

Let's recap the five ways to master response and responsibility: 1. Reassure your customer. Put the customer at ease so they know you are there to serve them and take care of them. 2. Respond quickly. Even if you can't solve the problem right away, start taking action so they can see it. 3. Respond positively. "I wish I could, but what I can do for you is …" 4. Take responsibility. Even if the problem isn't your fault, you are the one who must shoulder the apology. 5. Let the angry customer vent. It doesn't always feel good, but it's the right thing to do.

> 67% of consumers cite bad experiences as the reason they won't return to a business. You are 14 times more likely to sell to a current customer than a new one.

This section is going to take a more detailed look at how to turn around an irate customer. My clients come to me all the time and say, "What do I do when a customer's anger is all the way up to 11?" How do you deal with it when they're screaming at you, when they are beyond upset? How do you turn them around? There is a multistep process, and it is super simple.

Let's go back a moment. Do you remember the three things your customers want from you? Here's a reminder.

1. They want to feel heard.
2. They want to feel understood.
3. They want to feel cared for—even the ones who are furious.
4. It is going to take a lot of practice, so let's dive in.
5. *Let them vent.*

We briefly touched on this a few pages back, but what does it really mean? It means don't try to stop them. Don't contradict them. Let them have their say. You'll have to sit there and take it for a while, but it is so important that you do, because when somebody tells you why he or she is upset, and you respond with, "Well, that's not true"—even if you are right—how do you think the person feels? How will they react to that? If you say, "Sir, just calm down," will that calm them down? Does it ever calm them down? Probably not. It's dismissive. In that moment, it's best not to tell anyone to do anything. You can try, but it won't end well. You might be thinking that you need to keep control of the situation. You will be in control—trust me.

Maybe you've experience something similar. Have you ever had an argument with your spouse, your friend, or a family member, and you just let it go. Maybe you didn't feel like dealing with it then. What happened when you didn't deal with it? It probably festered like a sore.

Nine times out of 10, when you let an angry person vent, especially when you are in customer service, they are getting their anger out of their system. Wait in silence, and let the person finish. Don't say, "Are you done?" because that will just get them worked up all over again. A little silence is all that's needed. These customers just want to get what's bothering them off their chest. They want to be heard. They need that, and you need to provide that. Let them tell their story; let them get it out. You will find, more often than not, a calmness will follow after they finish. They might even go on to say that it was not your fault and that they just wanted the product or service to work. They may even end up saying, "Hey, I'm am sorry. I'm just really upset, you know?" Has something like that ever happened to you before? Just let them get it out.

*2. Let them know you understand.*

After the storm passes, you must be sympathetic, because the second thing a customer wants, from a psychology standpoint, is to be understood. Let them know that you understand. Just saying the simple words "I understand" or "I know that's frustrating," will be calming to them. We're going to talk about the best ways to sympathize with your clients.

*3. Let them know you will do everything you can to solve the problem.*

One way to do that is to recap the problem for them so they know you listened. Then, let them know you will help them. Tell them, "I promise to do everything I can to make this right for you." BOOM! Now you are clearly showing that you heard them, that you understand them, and that you care for them. Let them know you will do everything you can to help them.

*4. Use humor to diffuse a situation.*

This requires a little intelligence, wisdom, and timing. You have to be very careful when using humor to diffuse a situation. Not everyone shares the same sense of what's funny—for some it might sound flippant and get a customer riled up again. Here are some stories of successfully using humor to build brand loyalty and diffuse a situation.

There was a little boy who had some new Lego toys—those little action figures and blocks that you put together. He was going to lunch or breakfast with his family. His dad told him not to bring his Lego toy because he might lose it. Well, he brought it anyway … and he lost it. So, his dad, being the intelligent man that he is, said, "OK! You're going to write a letter to the customer service people telling them what you did." I can't remember the name of the Lego character, so let's call him Master Wizard. The kid wrote the letter, and a customer service representative actually responded—in character. He wrote, "I know you lost your Master Wizard." The letter continued, "We will find him. He must be on a mountain. But you must listen to your wise father. Don't worry, we'll send you another Master Wizard, but be careful and keep him in his kingdom."

The employee used humor appropriately. I can imagine the child's dad reading it, laughing, and smiling. I am paraphrasing the story, but you get the idea. Humor can be an effective tool to build loyal customers. There is another story about a travel company's social media customer service using humor with an angry customer. Someone on social media sent the company a request. Six months went by with no response, so the guy posts, "I haven't heard back from you guys in six months. You know what I could have done in six months?" The social media customer service rep responded, "I apologize," and started listing all the things the customer could have done in six months in Southeast Asia (where the company was located). You could have seen this sight, that sight, gone on a boat ride. He used humor to diffuse the situation. The person on the other end loved it and expressed that using "LOL" and other social media lingo. I'm paraphrasing again, but I want you to really understand that you can use humor with customers to great effect. It's about changing your customer's mindset, especially the really angry ones.

5. *Give the client unexpected added value.*

This is where the term "Wow your customer" comes from—and it's important. Added value could be something tangible, like a coupon, or it could be just kind words at the right time. It could be as simple as responding to something you heard them say when they were upset. Maybe they said, "I'm sorry for being angry, but my dog just passed away, and I'm so upset." Remember that, and let them know you're sorry, you sympathize, and that you hope everything turns out OK for the customer. For them, that might be an unexpected added value—they will know you really listened. If you work in a restaurant, you could say you're sorry that a meal wasn't satisfactory and offer the customer a coupon for a free meal, or even two coupons so they can bring someone with them. *That* is unexpected added value.

> Resolve a complaint in the customer's favor, and they will do business with you again 70% of the time.

Years ago, I had just bought a house and was getting ready to set up all the utilities, like the electricity and gas, etc. Back then, I was working from home, so it was very important for me to get the cable guys out there to install Internet service as soon as possible. I called the company, and the representative said a technician would be at my house that Monday morning. Well, Monday morning comes, no calls, no show. I call the company and ask the representative what happened. The rep said someone would be out there the next day. Tuesday comes. I sit, I wait, but nobody shows—again. Same thing Wednesday. Same thing Thursday. Nearly a whole week goes by, and nobody shows up to install my Internet. Unbelievable. I called them again on Friday, and I tell the representative that the situation is unacceptable. I was *really mad*. If I hadn't already ordered it, I would have switched cable companies that instant. The representative tells me, "We're going to get somebody out there this Monday morning for sure." A technician did finally come that morning, and the company did do a follow-up phone call to ask if everything was OK. I said, "Yes, I have Internet now. I'm not happy, but have Internet."

On Wednesday of that same week, there's a knock on my door. When I open it up, there was a delivery person with a box for me. I had just moved in, and I'm getting a delivery already! I signed for it, he hands me the box, and tells me who sent it. The cable company! I opened up the box, and guess what was inside? A box of cookies. There's a note inside, and it says, "Dear Mr. Brownlee. Welcome to our company. I know we messed up. We apologize. Please accept these cookies as our sincere apology. And thank you for remaining a customer." I couldn't believe it. *They sent me cookies.* When was the last time your cable company sent you cookies? I thought it was fantastic; it put a smile on my face. That's extra added value—and completely unexpected. How much does it cost to send some cookies? Not very much. They kept me as a client for a long time.

Ask yourself this question: What can you or your company do to give your clients unexpected added value? It doesn't have to be expensive. It just needs to be something that is sincere.

It's very important to remember that to help an irate customer, you must do these steps in order, like a recipe. Have you ever baked anything, like cookies? You have to work the recipe in order—first you mix together the sugar, flour, and butter for the dough, then you mix in the chocolate chips, then you plop the dough on a cookie sheet, and bake the cookies in the oven at a certain temperature for a certain amount of time. What happens if you put the chocolate chips in the oven first? It is not going to work, and you won't get any cookies. Customer service is like a recipe. You just can't go straight to humor, for example. You have to do everything in order.

> **66% of consumers who switched brands did so because of poor service.**

Let's recap. How can you turn around an angry customer? These are the five crucial steps—and they must be done in this order:

Let them vent. Let them have their say while you stay silent. Sometimes, it doesn't sound like they are ever going to stop yelling, but they will stop at some point.

Let them know you understand and sympathize with their issue.

Let them know you will do everything you can to solve it.

Use humor to diffuse a situation—but make sure you are using it appropriately—not flippantly—and at the right time.

Give the client unexpected added value.

Congratulations! You've made it through this very important chapter. Here are some exercises you can do on your own to reinforce what you learned in this section.

Exercise No. 1: Try some role-playing with a friend or spouse—even one of your kids. This exercise will really help drive this chapter home for you.

Partner A: Use a real-world example of an angry customer experience you dealt with in the past. Take on that person's vocal tone and facial expressions, even their volume—everything. I want you to complain to Partner B for one minute. Use a timer, and just unload on your partner.

Partner B: In this instance, you are the one who will practice letting them vent and turning that irate customer around with the appropriate response.

Then you and your partner will switch. Partner B will pretend to be a different client and unload on Partner A. Partner A will then practice letting them vent and turning around that irate customer with an appropriate response.

Exercise No. 2: I want you to think about the top three customer service challenges that have you most frequently experienced. Be specific. You are going to find patterns. What are the things frustrating people either with you, or your product or service? It could even be your industry. What challenges keep coming up?

Exercise No. 3: Using what you have learned in this program so far, list the best solution to overcome each of those challenges that you listed above—one at a time. This is important because it will help you figure out how to solve the challenges that keep coming up—the most *challenging* challenges. When can come up with a solution for those, you can go to work with more confidence because you will know exactly what to do. You'll have a game plan. This will help you become more successful and help give you a chance to create those raving fan clients by delivering world-class customer service. Anybody who does anything world-class takes the challenges they face and breaks them down to find their solutions.

*"To understand the man, you must first walk a mile in his moccasin."*
—NATIVE-AMERICAN PROVERB

*"Our attitude towards others determines their attitude towards us."*
—EARL NIGHTINGALE, RADIO SPEAKER AND AUTHOR

# 6

# EMPATHY IN CUSTOMER SERVICE

> 86% of consumers quit doing
> business with a company because of a
> bad customer experience.

We're now going to talk about Secret No. 6: Empathy in customer service.

You have learned in the preceding chapters how you build a foundation of empathy. You learned some skills and some strategies along the way. Empathy is a huge part of customer service, and it gives you a chance to show the world what you are made of.

What is empathy? Empathy is putting yourself in somebody else's shoes. You need to put yourself in your customer's shoes, and that can tough sometimes. Especially when we have all work with company procedures, rules, and regulations. We constantly have to refer to our manuals to find out whether or not they align with our customer service. Sometimes, we use the manuals as a crutch—a crutch that allows us to say "no." It's a crutch that allows us to say to a customer, "I am sorry. We can't do that for you. It's not our policy." It's an easy way out.

As customer service representatives, we really have to put ourselves in our customers' shoes so we can feel what they are feeling and experience what they are experiencing. I will give you an example. I have a cell phone contract with a big company that I don't really love, but I need my cell phone to communicate and get work done. I couldn't function without it. I was getting ready to go on a speaking tour and checked my cell phone bill before I left. I noticed there was a phone call to Australia for a few hundred dollars. I have always wanted to go there, but I don't actually know anyone there who I might call! Clearly, this item on the bill was a mistake because it happened during a time I was speaking at a seminar—that wasn't in Australia. I figured this was a simple mistake that should be easy to fix. So, I called them up to tell them what I found on my bill, and I get Mr. Robot Man. I tell him my problem, and he goes, "Ahhhhh," like he understands, followed by, "There is nothing I can do." "What do you mean there's nothing you can do? I didn't make this call. Can't you credit my bill? This phone call—that I didn't make—is a few hundred dollars. You've got to do something." Nothing. No response from this guy.

I think to myself, "OK. Let's try to bring out the human side of Mr. Robot Man." I ask him a question: "Has this ever happened to you with the phone company? He said yes. I said,

"OK, great. I am sure you were pretty upset. What did you do to solve it?" He says, "I paid it."

"That's your solution? You just paid it?" I could tell this transaction was going to be a dead end, so I hung up. Immediately after, I get a text survey asking me to rate my service. "How did we do? Rate us from zero to 10." I text back zero, zero, zero! I was so upset. About two days later, I get a phone call from the phone company. "We noticed you gave a really low rating for customer service from the text we sent you." I think, "Oh, this is good. My complaint was escalated. Now I am going to get this thing solved."

Boy, was I wrong. I could tell immediately that the representative on the phone was preparing for battle. She was ready for a fight. I told her what happened and asked again if the company could credit my account for the phone call, and she said, "No." She didn't provide even the bare minimum of customer service whatsoever. She was worse than Mr. Robot Man because she was clearly on the defensive.

I decided then that when I got back from my trip, I would change cell phone companies (though probably to another big company I won't like). That was my big strategy.

Before I went out to dinner that night, my phone rang. It's an 800 number. I pick it up, and a man starts speaking. "I understand you have been having some difficulty with our customer service department." I said, "Well, that's one way to put it."

He said, "I apologize. I am here now, and I promise to take excellent care of you. Just give me a few minutes to work on this thing, and we will get this phone call taken off the bill and get your account credited, and you will be good to go."

I replied, "This is great! This is absolutely unbelievable, but I am going to dinner right now, so can I call you back?"

He said, "Well, I wish I could, but you might get somebody else."

"OK. That's it! You are coming to dinner with me!"

I took him to the restaurant with me—on the phone, of course—and we went through everything, and we resolved it.

I told you at the beginning of this book that by providing world-class customer service, you will end up saving time. You will gain time. How many phone calls, how many conversations did it take to resolve my issue with this company? Three. Each of these calls was least 20 minutes long—so we were talking for about an hour in total. This big company is paying these three people for 20 minutes of their time. Depending on the problem, these customer service calls could be as long as 45 minutes! They are paying these people for their time to resolve an issue. The company could have empowered these employees so that the problem could be resolved in one phone call—the first one. This is what I want you to understand: When you improve your customer service to world-class customer service, you are going to save time because you do not have to keep dealing with the same angry customer. Get it resolved! Get it done.

I know you guys have got this, but I want to tell you another story to drive it home. I live by the beach. There is a boardwalk right by the Pacific Ocean, and my son and I went down there for a little father-son time. I am on my skateboard, and he's on his scooter. My son is 3 years old—and he is an ace on his scooter! Everyone stops to look at him—he is so good.

He says he is hungry, so we stop at this little food area where you can get a burrito. We are sitting there and eating when my son says, "Daddy! I'm thirsty. I want some water." I said OK. It was self-serve, and they had a little water jug and cups you could fill up the water. I am wiping off my hands and getting ready to get up and get the water, when suddenly a man comes up to us with a glass of water and sets it on the table. I look up and say, "Oh, hey, thank you so much!" He said, "I heard he needed some water, so I brought him some."

I said, "Great, are you a waiter?" He says, "Yes, I am."

"That's fantastic."

"But I'm not working right now."

Wow. An off-the-clock waiter comes and brings us water—just because he heard my son and me talking. He understood intuitively that we needed something. That's empathy. It turned out he didn't even work at this restaurant. He was just being nice. He was just a guy who was showing kindness and caring—for no other reason than my kid wanted some water. That is powerful.

Think about it: Just that little act of kindness and caring had a ripple effect. I mean, here I am talking about someone bringing us water. It was probably a little thing for him, but it made a lasting impression on me. He showed empathy, and that had a really lasting impact.

So, ask yourself how can you show empathy to your customers. When was the last time you did it? When was the last time you showed empathy toward your kids, or your significant other, or your family and friends?

Showing empathy should come naturally. If you have kids, and one of them has skinned his knee, you feel that pain, don't you? It's a natural thing for humans; we are empathetic beings. But for some reason we lose that empathy when we get to work—we cut off that part of ourselves from others. Make sure you open yourself up to showing empathy to your clients, because, as customer service representatives, we are building relationships with them.

> 40% of customers begin purchasing from a competitor because of their reputation for great customer service.
> 84% of organizations are now embracing the customer experience model.

In this section, we are going to look at the four keys to mastering empathy in customer service. We do it naturally with each other, and we need to make sure we are doing it with our customers and clients.

*1. Put yourself in your customer's shoes.*

This piece of advice goes double for the angry clients. Let them vent, let them unload, let them know they are being heard and that they are understood. Let them know that you are going to take care of them. Really try to understand where they're coming from, and ask yourself how you would feel or react if the same thing was happening to you. Doing this will give you a whole new level of understanding.

*2. Recall a time when you were in a similar situation.*

First, how did you feel while it was happening? When you were in a similar predicament, how should that issue have been handled? How would you have wanted someone to help you? When you are talking to an irate customer, share your story with them. Why? It will help build rapport. They will instantly think, "Oh, good! It's not just me. This has happened to you, too." They might even ask how you handled it.

When you share that story, you can really take control of what's happening. Sometimes clients are misinformed about how a situation should be handled, or they are misinformed about a policy. Whoever said that the customer is always right was wrong. It's great in theory, but it is not correct. Of course, you can't tell a customer, "You're wrong!" But you can say something like, "You know, when I was in a situation like this myself, I thought that it was x, y, and z, but then I found out it is actually a, b and c." Very nonthreatening, isn't it? This type of interaction can diffuse a situation because a light bulb goes off in a customer's head. They know you understand and are knowledgeable—and they will start listening to you.

*3. Show genuine concern for your customer's challenge.*

This applies regardless of the rules, regulations, and conditions that you have to enforce on behalf of your company. This will make your client feel cared for. This doesn't mean you go down the rabbit hole with them, but doing it the right way shows concern.

*4. Act appropriately.*

Is your response appropriate for this situation and the circumstances? For example, we've talked about smiling and eye contact, but if a customer is really upset and you keep smiling and smiling—that's only going to irritate them and get old really quick. Read the room—act appropriately and respond appropriately.

I worked with a client who provides emergency roadside assistance. Imagine you're a mom with two kids, and your car breaks down while you're driving in the middle of a huge storm. The person you call in that moment is the most important person in your life, because they are the only ones who can help you. If you're on the other end of the line, you want to respond appropriately to that mother. Show concern, show empathy, and put yourself in their shoes. How would you feel? How would you want somebody to handle the situation? It is one small shift in your perception, but it is going to really change how you respond to that person. You want to show this mom that you understand, you want to show them comfort, and you want them to know you will help. You might also say something like, "I will make sure that you are taken care of" or "I will make sure that the tow truck gets to you ASAP, and I'm going to stay on the phone with you until that happens." In a different customer service situation, you might tell an angry customer "I under-stand" or "I would feel the same way" or "I can imagine how that would be frustrating" or "I will make sure that you are happy, excited, and more than satisfied with our solutions."

These are great opportunities to recall a similar situation and share it with the customer. "I can relate because I experienced x, y, and z." You will build that commonality, that rapport, which will make them listen to you and look to you for the answer.

A customer service representative's worst fear is that they will lose control of a phone call or transaction, but you are always in control. By showing genuine concern, you stay in control in a very subtle and ethical way. Trust me, you *are* in complete con-trol when you are showing sincere empathy for that person.

✳ ✳ ✳

In this section, we are going to illustrate even more clearly how important empathy is. I really want you guys to get this because this can change your whole business. This can change your whole customer experience. I call this the "window of perception."

Here is the concept: If you and your customer are looking through a window at each other, what do you see? Let's say you are inside of a house. Here, you are surrounded by your furniture and belongings, but when you look out the window, you see the front lawn, the street in front of your house, and you see the homes on the other side of the street. When your customer is outside looking in, they see the sidewalk, they see the picket fence, but when they look through the window where you are, they see your surroundings. Polar opposites. The customer sees inside, and you see outside.

So, what has this got to do with customer service? When your customer calls with an issue or problem, they can only see it from the outside, they can only see what has happened to them. On the other side, you are in your office, and you've got your procedures, manuals, rules and regulations, your different customer service strategies. You might even have product knowledge—knowing things contribute to the solution. What you see is completely different. In order to come up with the best solutions for your customers and your clients, you have to step outside and see things from your customer's point of view. In other words, when you look through that window now, you have to see exactly what the customer sees. That's the only way you are going to find the best solution faster and more easily. If you stay on your side of the window, what are the chances of that problem being solved? Very slim. You need to see the solution from both sides of the window and help the customer meet you in the middle.

Let's recap.

Make sure that you put yourself in your customer's shoes. That is the only way to learn empathy. Empathy is something that comes naturally to people in their daily lives and something you can bring into your workplace—with your customers, with your clients, with your co-workers. If somebody has a problem they need solved or a task they need completed, don't shove them off. Empathize with them. Find out what kind of pressure are they under, and take the time to really understand. Make sure that they feel heard and cared for. Don't forget about your internal customers—your co-workers. Empathy works with them, too. Empathy will make your life and their lives a lot easier and create a more enjoyable workplace.

Recall your own experiences with customer service. Ask yourself how would you feel and react in such a situation or how you reacted. How did you want somebody to solve the situation for you?

Show genuine concern for your customer's challenge. Really show them that their challenge is important to you.

And you always want to act appropriately. Read the room. Don't smile if the situation calls for concern and seriousness. You don't want to smile while somebody is in the midst of a crisis. React appropriately.

Remember the window of perception. It is a great way to illustrate what happens every single day in customer services. The customer is on one side of the window looking in, while the customer representative is on the other side looking out. As a customer service representative, you need to come over to their side of the window and see what they are seeing and feel what they are feeling. That way, you can meet them in the middle.

Here are some exercises that you can do at home using your journal.

Exercise 1: Describe a challenge or a struggle that you had, either personally or professionally, in which someone helped you through it with kindness and caring. Did they listen to you? Did they let you vent? Did they understand you? I want you to write the answers in your journal. Dig up that memory and put yourself back in that situation. What did you see? What did you hear? What did you feel? Describe the struggle you were having in detail.

Exercise 2: Describe what specifically that other person did to help you through the challenge at that time?

Exercise 3: Describe how you can apply those specific things that person did to help you to create a world-class customer service experience for your clients—for both internal and external clients. We are connecting our brains to solutions for challenges that you face every day and have experienced in your own lives.

We will talk more about that in the remaining chapters, but I really want you to be able to put the information that you've learned in this book to practice.

Exercise 4: You need a partner for this one. Try this with a co-worker. If you are a "solopreneur," find a friend, or maybe one of your children, your spouse, or significant other to help. This exercise is really important, so don't skip it!

Partner A and B should describe challenges they have faced. Partner B should then describe the challenge that you talked about while Partner A uses empathy, kindness and caring to help partner B feel heard understood and cared for.

This exercise is awesome and eye opening. Give it a try!

*"In order to move mountains for customers, you have to be clear on which one they want you to move."*

—DAVID BROWNLEE

*"The key is to set realistic customer expectations, and then not to just meet them, but to exceed them—preferably in unexpected and helpful ways."*

—RICHARD BRANSON, INVESTOR AND PHILANTHROPIST

CHAPTER

7

# CLARIFY, CLARIFY, CLARIFY!

> 78% of surveyed customers say that competent customer service reps are most responsible for a happy customer experience.

I n this chapter, we delve into Secret No. 7—clarify, clarify, clarify! It is so important in customer service to make sure you're working on the right things for your customers. I bet this has happened to you many times: A customer tells you their problem, and you begin working on a remedy. When you finally have one, and you bring it to the customer, they say to you, "That wasn't the problem. This is what my problem is. That's not what I really meant." This scenario has definitely happened to me. I had to learn the hard way how important it is to clarify.

Several years ago, when I had my entertainment company, we would do live special events all over the world. This particular year, we were so blessed to be able to work an NBA All-Star party in Los Angeles. All the big names were there—we even had NFL football players. We had three or four stages. We had talent on all the stages. We handled everything from the security to the Porta Potties. It was a really big deal for us. And it was an awesome event; everybody had a great time. But this event really taught me the importance of clarification. My client told me to put together an area for vendors with booths that would be set up so the vendors could be visible to the guests. I was the point person for that, and I had contracted with companies for tents and tables. It should point out here that there were no backs on the tents. It turned out that was the one thing I didn't clarify with the client hosting the party—whether or not they wanted backs on the tents. It turned out they did. In fact, it was they who asked me where the backs to the tents were, and I said I didn't order any. This was a huge sticking point for them, and I didn't clarify what the client wanted.

You have to learn from your mistakes. That event went off without a hitch, and everything was fixed on time, but the client wanted something specific. The fact that I didn't clarify something with them was a huge setback that cost us time. So now, every time I talk to a client, I write everything down. Writing things down saves time, and it also helps you deliver an experience that helps build a relationship—which is what I've been talking about throughout this book. When I visit with new companies to train them, I ask them what is the most important thing they want to learn during their customer service training. They tell me, and I write it down in the order that they tell me because the first thing anyone tells you is the thing that is most important to them. I write it down, then the next thing, then the next, and so on. Make sure you write it down and you clarify afterwards. If you don't feel comfortable writing in a certain situation at least make sure you're actively listening (which we also discussed in an earlier chapter). Then repeat it back to the client.

✳ ✳ ✳

In this section, we're going to look at the three keys to excellent clarification in customer service.

**The first key is verbally repeating the customer's request back to the customer.** If you've been to a fast-food joint recently, you might have notice that they're using a lot of new technology. Now, when you pull up to a drive-thru, there is a screen that displays your order. You say, "I will have a little heart attack in a box and a little cholesterol in a bag," and the person taking your order will repeat exactly what you said, and then it will *also* appear on the screen so you can see it before you pull up to the window to pay.

You would think this is a foolproof way to avoid order errors, but you can still get a bag with the wrong food and only find out after you've driven 20 miles away. But these screens are a vast improvement from previous years. They were put in place because fast-food restaurant companies realized that they needed a better way to clarify these orders because they had some angry customers with a fish sandwich instead of a burger. The fact is, if you're a fast-food joint, it's your business to get the orders right. You want to deliver a quality solution—and that requires clarity. Once you understand the customer's needs and desires, and you clarify these with the customer, make sure you get it right. And repeating the request is how you begin to ensure a good customer service experience.

It doesn't take very long to do, but very few companies do this first step. Make sure you repeat the request because sometimes a client may say, "No, that's not what I meant." Clarifying that on the front end will save you time and help you deliver world-class customer service. It doesn't always feel that way, but it saves you a ton of time overall.

> **3 in 5 Americans would try a new brand or company for a better service experience.**

**The second key is to confirm the customer's desired outcome.** This is so important, but very few companies do this. Not only do you want to clarify the customer's request, you also want to know what their end goal is. Why is this deadline or that delivery day so important? You want to know because the journey toward reaching that desired outcome may or may not happen exactly how the customer expects it to. Delays or mistakes can happen because of your company procedure or policy—or any number of factors. Often, customers will get caught up in the minutia of what they want and get stuck in outcome they're envisioning.

When something like this happens, you might say, "I understand that you are upset, but here is what I want you to know: If we do it this other way, we *can* get to your desired outcome." Chances are the customer will react well. "OK. That's not how I wanted to get there, but as long as we get there, I'm happy."

Knowing the client's end game will help you reach an agreeable solution that works for everyone. In order to do that, you have to confirm the desired outcome.

Here's an example: I have a coaching client who has a retail business that receives a lot of goods from overseas. He brings in shipping containers, and once he gets those products, he redistributes them to his clients here in the U.S. In the beginning, he was really frustrated—and so were his customers—because he guaranteed that his company could deliver in 30 days. But guess what? Sometimes it took 45 days! He had to tell his U.S. clients that the products would be a few weeks late, which made them really angry. I told my friend that he should start telling them that they will get the product within 60 days.

Most of the time, the containers would be on time and within the 30-day delivery period. But by clarifying with his clients that the timing might be closer to 60 days, he was better able to manage their expectations. And if the shipment came early—he would call and tell them that, and it made him look like a rockstar! By changing the timing on his guarantee, he was able to better clarify that timing with his customers help them with their desired outcome. By rethinking your process, you have eased the deadline burden on your workload, made yourself look good, and made your client happy. The client feels cared for, they think, "Wow! These guys are awesome! They always over-deliver, and they are crazy fast. These guys went from zero to hero." Now this client has a working customer service business model that he can enjoy with a lot less pressure because he is able to meet those deadlines and keep his customers informed.

**The third key is to repeat the solution.** Let's suppose somebody is really upset, but you have come up with the remedy. Make sure the client fully understands—100 percent—what that solution is. Like many people, sometimes a client is only passively listening and might not catch everything you told them—and then blame you later. I'm sure you've heard this before: "That's not what you told me." Make sure your customer is listening by repeating the solution and confirming that they understand what you told them.

Do this on the front end. For example, while placing an order for a client, make sure they understand which product they will be receiving. Sometimes a customer may order the model number A1, when really they wanted model number A2. To clarify with the customer, say something like, "So, you wanted the A1 that includes x, y, and z? Is that what you're looking for?" They may answer with, "No, I wanted the one with the extra a, b, and c"—which turns out to be model number A2. That small act of repeating the order or solution just saved yourself and the client a lot of time and aggravation.

> According to consumers, customer service agents failed to answer their questions 50% of the time.

I once held a customer service training workshop for a big international brand—a celebrity brand. I worked closely with its customer service team. During the holidays, this company ships out a lot of products. And like most big companies, there are some problems with the process that they can't control. During the holidays, everyone is shipping products. You have all these big companies trying to provide next-day delivery all at the same time. Some even offer same-day service. Usually companies plan for this seasonal crunch and warn their customers via an email or message on their websites that say will say something like, "Please expect longer shipping times." Some companies will even make a phone call. "We just wanted to let you know that during the holiday season another day or two might be added to your delivery time. Order on time so you can get it on time."

If you work in a business like this, and a client calls you to order a product during the holidays, it pays to remind them about delays. For example, "I know that you wanted this item and that you have asked for the two-day shipping. However, if it gets there in three or four days, is that going to work for you?" Deal with the potential for delays on the front end because dealing with it on the back end could result in a negative transaction. You are going to save yourself time and aggravation on both ends of the transaction.

Clarifying the conditions of a transaction with a customer or client shows that you care for your clients, and that clarification might even get your company extra sales because you made a point of managing expectations.

That's a lot of information, so let's do a quick recap. The

three keys to clarification in customer service are: 1. Repeat the request. Clarifying what the customer wants up front will save you time. 2. Confirm the desired outcome. Work with your client on alternative solutions if necessary. 3. Repeat the solution. Make absolutely sure they know what they're going to get so you can stop a potential problem before it happens or come up with a solution to one more quickly.

A couple of sections ago we talked about how to turn around an irate customer. What turns those people into raving fan clients who never want to leave you is when you can take that angry emotion and turn it into a positive emotion. Clarification is a huge part of turning a situation like that around.

As a customer service professional, you have to be clear about the solutions for your client and what their desired outcome is. When companies began experiencing holiday shipping problems, they realized that telling the clients and the customers that delivery could take an extra day or two was the right thing to do. The simple task of asking, "Is that OK with you?" made the customer feeling in control. You can't always control when a product will be shipped or delivered, but by coming up with solutions on the front end to manage expectations, it saves you time on the back end.

✶ ✶ ✶

In this section, I am going to give you tools to reinforce the lessons in the previous section on clarification. You might be wondering what you can say to customers to help with the clarification process. I am going to give you some phrases to help you get started. Play around with them, and work on coming up with some of your own.

The first key, you'll remember, is repeating the customer's request. Doing this will show the customer that you are listening. Clarification up front helps avoid confusion when you try to resolve problems, and clarification is going to ensure that you are working on the customer's actual problem. I know this has happened to you before—you're trying to move mountains to solve someone's problem, and, at the very end when you think everything is settled, they tell you that it wasn't the problem they needed fixed. You just wasted a ton of your time that you won't get back. Do it on the front end, repeat the customer request word for word to show that you are listening. Clarification will help you solve the problem and come up with a solution.

Try saying, "To confirm: You're looking for x, y, z" or "You would like to x, y, z."

The second key is to confirm the desired outcome. If a client is not excited about your solution, what do you do? Remember when I talked about how important it is to take verbal and nonverbal cues? Let's suppose you ask this question: "What would be an outstanding resolution for this issue?" Nine out of 10 times, they won't say anything. If this happens, it's at this point you can tell them what you are willing to offer. Don't sweep the silence under the rug. A lot of the time, customer service representatives will realize too late that their client is upset because the customer didn't respond to their question, "Do you understand, and are you OK with the outcome?" Remember, 96 percent of your angry customers will not tell you that they are upset, and 91 percent just won't come back.

Here are some examples of confirming the desired outcome.

"Let me get this clear: What you ultimately want is x, y, z."

"If I can do (customer's desired outcome), would that be an excellent solution for you?"

"If I could give you a full refund, would that be an excellent solution for you?"

Finally, the third key is repeating the solution—and all of its details—so the customer fully understands what you're offering and what you have agreed on. Judge their reaction to the solution by picking up on their verbal and nonverbal cues.

For example, you might ask them, "How do you feel about that?" Hopefully, they'll be honest with you, and you can get a verbal assurance of their satisfaction. Many companies won't clarify any details of any part of a transaction, and even the companies that do clarify typically use only one of the three keys. Usually they will repeat the request, but they won't clarify the desired outcome or repeat the solution. You need all three to provide excellent customer service.

Here are some exercises you can do in your spare time to work on reinforcing the lessons you learned in this chapter.

For a full week, practice clarification by using the three keys you've learned in this chapter. Do it for every customer you come in contact with that week. Write down what worked and what didn't work, and track your results in a journal. Get in the habit of using these tools, because it will become clear very quickly what works for you personally, for your company, and for your industry. You will create tools that are customized for your business.

Outside of the work environment, practice clarifying and

repeating solutions with your friends and your family, or businesses you frequent—do this as a customer yourself and with anyone else you come in contact with. Do that for a week and track your results in a journal. You may be surprised by what you discover. Make a mental note of the things that worked and keep doing them—practice them over and over.

*"Quality in a service or product is not what you put into it. It is what the client or customer gets out of it."*

—PETER DRUCKER, MANAGEMENT CONSULTANT

*"Don't find customers for your products, find products for your customers."*

—SETH GODIN, AUTHOR

CHAPTER

# SOLUTIONS IN CUSTOMER SERVICE

We've reached the final chapter—and now we are going to discuss Secret Number 8: Solutions. As a customer service representative, your goal is to provide solutions. There are two kinds of solutions that help you deliver world-class customer service.

**The first kind is fulfilling a request.** A customer has called or come in to your business, and they want to buy or use your product or service. Nothing is wrong, they just want you to fulfill their need at that moment—because every legitimate product or service overcomes a challenge they are having. Even if a customer only wants a stick of gum, there are challenges that come with that—what flavor, what brand, how many do they want—and the solution is in how you help get them the gum they want to satisfy their sweet tooth. If there is a legitimate product or service, there will be a challenge, and it's up to you to provide a solution.

**The second kind of solution is finding a remedy.** When your customer has a problem with you or a problem with your company or your product or your service, you need to help fix the problem and make it right.

To do accomplish these two types of solutions, you'll need to bring everything you've learned to the table. I will teach you how to use all the tools in this book to assess any situation for a successful solution. You are going to ask questions, clarify what they want and/or need, and read their verbal and nonverbal cues. Are you guys starting to connect the dots? Then let's charge ahead!

I'm going to tell you a story about solutions and leverage. We discussed leverage in a preceding chapter. The world keeps coming up with all these great inventions and technology. It seems like every six months, there's some new and amazing product or service in the marketplace. I am on the road traveling all the time, and a few years back a friend of mine asks me why I'm still taking taxis everywhere. He tells me about this smart-phone app called Ride Share. Think about all the problems that come with taking taxis: First and foremost, it's the drivers. They are rude. Second, cab companies charge you a ton of money. The cabbies will take you down side streets so the meter can keep running, and they will deliberately drive in heavy traffic so they can make a couple of extra bucks out of you. If you've got luggage with you, you'll be lucky if they bother to pop the trunk open let alone put the stuff into the trunk for you. Years ago, cabdrivers actually had a newspaper for you and some good conversation; they got your bags for you, and they were on top of things. But times have changed.

My buddy tells me about Ride Share. He tells me that sometimes they have a cold bottle of water for you; some even have snacks and newspapers. The drivers are friendly and always smiling. Imagine the last time you saw a cabdriver smile! These drivers will come get your bags if they are local, they'll tell you about what's going on in the city at the time. This sounded promising.

I had a speaking event in Miami. Before I left, I downloaded the app and was ready to use it, and … nothing! A message came up that said the app was unavailable due to some union strike. I ended up taking a cab. No surprise, the driver was already upset before I got in the taxi, and he didn't help me with my bags—though he did manage to pop open the trunk for me, but that was it. He didn't speak to me the whole trip (which, I guess was OK). We get to the destination, and I decide to pay with my credit card, but the driver asks me if I have cash. I say no and ask why it matters, because he has the credit card machine installed in his car, which means I could be out of his hair pretty quickly. Instead, the guy got mad at me for wanting to give him a credit card. He was screaming at me. He just went nuts. I looked at him shocked, and then finally he says, "Take your card and get out." I tell him I want to pay. He says, "No! Get out." I say, "Okie docile." He pops open the trunk, I get my bags, and I went on my merry way. The good news is I got a free ride. The bad news is I had to put up with that guy.

That speaking engagement was sometime around the holidays, and the weather around the country was terrible, so hundreds of passengers were stuck at the airports. At the San Diego airport, where I was returning home, there was a long line to get a taxi, so I tried my app again—and it worked! Four minutes later, here comes this big black SUV. The driver gets out and greets me with a smile. He says, "Hey! How are you doing? Are you David? My name is John. Let me grab your bags." He opens up the door for me. Inside, he had bottles of water and a newspaper sitting there. It was awesome! He put all my stuff in the trunk, got back in the car and said, "Where are you coming in from? You must be tired. Do you want some music?" He made sure that I was comfortable as he drove me home. It was the best experience I'd had in years. What I love most about these types of services that use phone apps, like Ride Share, is that the customer has a voice! I get to see how many stars the driver has and I get to rate the service in real time. I gave him five stars, and left him a message. These types of reviews give the drivers leverage to perform at their best.

Here is a question is for supervisors, managers, and business owners: What kind of leverage are you giving your customer service representatives to make sure they can deliver world-class service and world-class solutions?

Here are a few examples of what to say to help offer solutions to your customers:

"Is there anything else that I can do for you?" You might have heard this one before at the grocery store, on the phone. I love this one. As customers, we've gotten so used to hearing that one that we might not always give an answer, but for a customer service representative, that question gives you a chance to wait for verbal cues or nonverbal cues. Also, have a creative and special solution for your customers, and evaluate the delivery of your solution. Ask yourself if it was creative and special enough for a great experience for that customer. If not, then next time try to do something that will really add extra value.

✷ ✷ ✷

In this section, we're going to look at the three keys to providing world-class solutions:

The first key comes in two parts: **The first is delivering the best-suited product and service or the best-quality product or service, and the second part is doing that with 100-percent accuracy**—not just a physical delivery but all the pieces that make up the whole. These two things together combine to help you come up with a solution that includes the right product or service for the customer, one that meets all of their needs.

Let's start with delivering the best product or service. If it's delivery, deliver it on time or deliver it early. Remember in the last chapter, we talked about managing expectations. If something will take 45 days to get arrive, tell the customer 60 days so it looks to them like you delivered it early.

You want the best-quality product or service that will exceed their expectations. The Ride Share app is a good example of that. It suited me, because I needed transportation, and I wanted an affordable and friendly service. I got all that and more.

You want to give your customer the best remedy that you can provide. Sometimes, a business will have a monthly special for customers, one that is also an incentive for employees. You've seen them: If you sell this product or that product, you'll get a commission. But before you make that sale, make sure it is best suited for your customer and that it is the best-quality product or service that will exceed their expectations.

Accuracy is the second part. You are must strive for 100-percent accuracy in completing a customer's request. You absolutely must deliver an accurate order. Let's go back to the fast-food example from Chapter 7. As I described, employees manning the window may clarify your order but still deliver the wrong items. You want to make sure you delivered the right food. You might even check what's in the bag yourself before you hand it over to the customer.

A few years ago, I worked with an international company that makes trophies. It operated in the U.S. and Asia. What challenges was this company facing? Well, it had thousands of clients from all over the world, and used an elaborate system to complete orders. The company began noticing an accuracy problem with the orders, so they had to go through each step of the system and check where the errors were happening. They had to make sure that they were putting a quality-assurance system in place that would improve accuracy. I am going to go back to the Ride Share example: When you enter in your destination, the application tells you how many miles it's going to be and how much they are going to charge. Unlike a cab, I don't have to hope and pray that the driver is going to take the fastest route. I know the route he is going to take; there is a map showing me the route. It really does deliver a solution that I am looking for.

Ask yourself about your business: Are you delivering something that is the best quality. Do you deliver that product with accuracy? Get honest. If one of those pieces is lacking, you have to get together with your team and start thinking about how you can improve. That's where innovation comes in, and I'm going to get into that in an upcoming section.

**The second key is anticipating your customer's needs.** This will help you get closer than ever to your customers and clients. So, close, in fact, that you tell them what they need before they realize it themselves. Steve Jobs is a perfect example of a leader who was brilliant at selling consumers stuff they didn't even know they needed. How can you do that? You can review your customers' purchase histories and make suggestions based on what you learn. Amazon is the *best in the world* at anticipating a customer's needs. The online retailer has designed a business technology around purchase history. If you've been on Amazon, you know that the website will often provide links that say, "You recently purchased this. You might want to buy this" or "In the past you got this. Here is the newer version that may be useful to you." Look at your customers' purchase histories.

You can also suggest a companion item that would complement the item they just bought. I am always buying toys on Amazon, and there is one thing that daddy always forgets to buy—batteries. It doesn't matter if I'm on Amazon or in a brick-and-mortar store. The good businesses will say, "Hey! Do you want some batteries with this thing?" Of course I do! I now have everything I need, and my kids can play with the toys right away—and it makes daddy look like a rockstar.

You may ask, "It's great for sales, but how does that apply to customer service?" As a customer, it subconsciously makes you feel like the company knows you. If the item you're suggesting is something that has value to the customer, they will personally feel cared for. You can make a customer feel understood and cared for—and you may not even need to talk to them. That's why your strategy and your company's strategy are so important. When you have a company-wide customer service philosophy, and you have a strategy in place, you can take care of this even when you are not talking face to face with your clients. And that is really cool.

**The third and final key: Alert the customer to the new and improved versions of the product or service that are currently available.** A lot of times companies will distribute surveys that ask what could be better about this product. Customers will give their feedback, and the company will use that information for developing updates and new products. They will make all the improvements and then release another version—like a 2.0. You've got to let your clients know about the new version. For example, this book is based on the 2.0 version of my training program. I took all the feedback that I received from my clients and viewers, I put all the things you're reading now into the new version of that program, then I let my clients know about it. A company should always ask itself what it can do to improve its services and products—and then offer it to their clients. They *will* appreciate it.

Offering new products can be uncomfortable for customer service reps. People are raised to be humble, so this act can seem to go against that upbringing. I see customer service reps who don't want to offer a customer the new product for fear the customer might think they getting up-sold. But if you have built a rapport, if you have built that relationship—and you honestly want to help your client overcome his or her challenge or issue or problem with whatever solution you provide—changing your mindset and getting over that discomfort will make it a lot easier to help people.

Lastly, I want to talk a little more about follow-up. We covered this a bit earlier in the book, and this is a topic I struggle with. Once I deliver my service or my product, so much happens after that sale or service. We get caught up in finishing the transaction, or we are on to the next customer. We have to remember to follow up with those customers whom we have already served. We're going to talk about some strategies for doing that—because this is truly where the magic happens. When you follow up with your customers in the correct way, it will generate referrals and turn customers into raving fan clients that will never leave you, and that, in turn, will increase revenues. I'll show you exactly how to do it in the next section.

Let's recap. Here are the three keys to providing world-class solutions:

You have to deliver the best-suited product and service and the best-quality product or service with 100 percent accuracy.

You have to anticipate a customer's needs. Look at customers' purchase histories and anticipate what they might need to help them on their journey. Anticipate a companion item, something that's going to complement the item or items they may have just purchased.

Alert the customer to new and improved versions of products or services they may have purchased in the past.

> 11% of customer loss could be prevented by simple company outreach. 95% of customers share bad experiences with others.

In this section, we are going to look at how to successfully ask for referrals. What if there was a way you could double your referrals this month? I have done it; my clients have done it—and now it's your turn. It is possible. In order to get to this section of them, the foundation had to be laid. You had to get honest, you had to learn about leverage, and you had to learn the skills of empathy. Now, it all comes together. When you get referrals, your business will never be the same again—in a good way!

As I mentioned in the previous section, this change starts with the follow-up—that's the beginning of getting to the referral process. You're going to have clients who are so happy—they will be over the moon—with your service that they are going tell all of their friends. They will write reviews on the many Internet sites and smart-phone review apps, and they will tell everybody how great you are. You can use all of the strategies you learned in this book and implement them to take your customer service and your company to another level. Trust me, when all of these strategies come together, you really can—politely and with confidence—ask for referrals and get them. This is what elevates businesses.

What do you do if you are a brick-and-mortar retail location or you have an office? You follow up right then and there at the end of a transaction. Ask the customer how the service was—and that's when you look for those verbal and nonverbal cues. If you own or work at a restaurant or any kind of retail location—maybe you sell clothing, for example—you want to ask right there because not everybody is going to say that they had a great experience. Try to dig deeper—politely and with confidence. With any luck, they will be honest.

You can follow up via email. You might want to try conducting a survey. Companies send out surveys all the time. That said, a survey must be administered correctly to get results! My biggest pet peeve with many company surveys is … *they're too long*! I get so annoyed when I click on a link to the survey only to find out it's the first page of a 120 pages—and some are ridiculously complicated! If you're like me, you say, "I'm out!" Maybe somebody has time to do this, but it's not me. If your company is sending out this kind of survey … STOP NOW!

Here is all you need for a survey. It's short and simple:

"On a scale from 1 to 10, how would you rank our customer service?" (If it is less than 10, add one more question: "What changes would you suggest?")

"What do you like best about a product or service?"

"Is there anything else you want us to know?"

That is it. That is all you need, and it will take your clients five minutes or less to fill out that survey. You can take that information and improve your product or your service, or anything about the way you do business. And definitely follow up on negative responses to your survey. Reach out to those clients—by phone or by email—and ask how can you make it better and make it right. Follow-up is important and requires putting a system in place to review the survey quickly after it's been submitted. Use that feedback to take action to improve your service. Respond to complaints immediately and provide creative remedies that will allow those customers to feel special. This is what will turn them into raving fan client that will never leave you.

Follow up on the phone. I call these "customer care calls." These calls have the biggest impact on my business as well as my clients' businesses. Create a database using either customer relationship management (CRM) software or even just a simple spreadsheet. It doesn't matter how many clients you have, just get their names, phone numbers, and email addresses. Also, make a note of what they purchased. Then either you or an employee should call these customers and ask how their service was. You could say, "Thank you for doing business with us! How was our service? Is there anything we can do to improve it?" Or you might say, "Hi! I am calling to check in with you and see how everything went with our product or service. We want to take excellent care of you." Wow! People love that. You want referrals and more business, and more and more money—this is the way to do it. If you're the person at the other end of the line, it just feels great to know a business wants to know your opinion.

I will give you an example. There is a rental car company that I love because they built a multibillion-dollar company based on customer service and customer experience. Some time ago, I returned a rental car to this company. That same day, after I got home from dropping it off, my phone rings. It's the rental car company. The first thing that went through my mind was that something was wrong with the car.

The representative on the line says, "I'm calling because I just wanted to make sure everything went well with you and your rental car. How was everything?"

I said, "Everything was great! Thanks for asking." Nobody had ever asked me that before.

They said, "Great! If you need another rental car in the future please let us know."

I hung up the phone. I was shocked but also happy some-body actually cared enough to give me a call to see how my transaction went. It was a short phone call, maybe 20 to 30 seconds at most, but it went a long way toward make me a raving fan customer—so much so that I am using this com-pany as an example right now. You can achieve the exact same result for you or your company. It's all about the team. I found out that this rental car company has its employees make those phone calls before they go home. At the end of every shift, the employees on that shift talk to the people whose rentals came in that day. You can do the exact same thing. Make those customer care calls, because that's the time to ask them for referrals!

You can also follow up via text message or other cell phone

technology. There are a lot of software platforms that allow you to send a text messages to your customers with a built-in survey, and there are also features you can get now that will turn your cell phone into a card reader that can also produce surveys. I was at the airport not too long ago, and I stopped to get a shoeshine. The employee pulls out his cell phone with this little white attachment sitting on top. I swiped my credit card, and it asked for my email address. After I entered it, my receipt was displayed, and there was a happy face and a frowning face on the receipt. The guy asked me how my service was that day. He was a nice guy, so ... happy face! It was powerful feedback for that service representative. I was happy, but what would have happened if I had clicked the frowning face? Well, he had my email address, so he could email me and ask me what he could have done to make the transaction go better. He could follow up easily. It was a simple thing that took me one touch of a button.

The text message survey works this way: I was on the phone with a company recently, and at the end of the phone call, I got a text message almost immediately that read, "Would you be interested in taking a one-question survey?" I replied yes, and I got another text asking whether or not I would hire this customer service representative to work for me. I'm a customer service coach, so I thought this question was genius. The person was good, so I texted back "YES." This company is getting a ton of insight from a simple one-question survey. I tell that story to business owners, managers, and supervisors to drive home the point that a survey does not have to be the length and difficulty of a college exam in order to get valuable information you can use raise your customer service from ordinary to world-class.

You can also follow up via the U.S. Postal Service. You might think nobody sends anything through the mail anymore—and you'd be right. But here's another ninja secret: If you want to reach somebody, and you are having a hard time getting them to respond to your emails or phone calls, send them something in the mail. I suggest sending them a little card. Remember when we were kids, and we would get a card in the mail—maybe for a birthday or a holiday, maybe from your grandparents or your uncle with a $100 bill inside? It was a great feeling, right? Take the time to follow up by writing to a customer and including a little incentive inside, something like, "Thank you for choosing us. Here is a coupon for your next visit. Please tell us how we did." You could even include the URL to a survey online. "Via mail" is not a crowded place anymore, which makes it a noticeable and great way to follow up. And the customers will love it!

Social media is another great way to get feedback. There are more and more customer service representatives on social media and on fan pages. Make sure you have a customer service professional monitoring that page constantly and is given the tools to be able to respond to questions and complaints.

Here are the most current social media statistics, and they are going up every day:

1. 46% of online customers expect brands to provide customer service on Facebook.
2. 83% of complaints that received a reply on social media liked or loved the fact that the company responded.

3. 88% of consumers are less likely to buy from companies that leave complaints on social media unanswered.
4. 70% of companies ignore customer complaints on Twitter.
5. Customers are 70% more likely to purchase from a brand they follow on Twitter.
6. More than 1 million people view tweets about customer service every week, and roughly 80% of customer service tweets are negative or critical in nature.

Lastly, you can also respond to your customers via a chat software platform. More and more companies use this platform to deliver a customer service experience. You can apply all the strategies that we've talked about in this book so far to chat transactions and provide and terrific customer experience. But here's the key to customer service via chat: Get to the point and solve the problem quickly. When I've tried to use chats to address a problem, a lot of the time it can be really frustrating. Sometimes, I have a simple question that requires a quick and simple answer. But after I put in my name, my email, and my account number, the representative will just start asking a bunch of questions that have nothing to do with the problem I need solved, prolonging the frustration. So, remember: When you're doing great customer service via chat, get to the point and solve the problem quickly.

Let's do a quick recap on follow-up. You can follow up at the location, via email, on the phone, via text message and other cell phone technology, U.S. mail, social media, and using chat software.

So … here's the million-dollar question: "What do I say

when I am asking for a referral?" We're going to get deep into that in the next section.

★ ★ ★

If you've applied all that you've learned in this book, before you know it you the referrals will start pouring in—especially as you continue to raise the bar with your customers. But how do you politely ask somebody for referrals? In this section, you're going find out. You have a golden opportunity to ask for a referral when you complete a successful customer care call that ends with a happy result. You want to make sure that you lead with, "How are you? Did I deliver for you? Did my company deliver for you? Are you happy?"

The customer is not always right, but they should always leave happy, and once we have established that everything is great, it's at that point we have the perfect opportunity to ask for a referral. You also have a wealth of opportunity to use your database that lists past clients and current clients—these are great prospects for new business. And, if you have a CRM that tracks customer calls, you can reach out to those people who maybe didn't buy a product or service from you at the time because maybe the timing wasn't right. Call them, too, because now may be in a better time for them. Even if you reach them and it's still not the right time, treat them with kindness and caring, and give them a world-class experience that will still make them want to recommend you to their friends and family.

People tell me all the time that asking for referrals just seems kind of forward and that they don't want to come off to "salesy." We are all naturally humble people, and we don't want to be pushy or rude. But let me tell you, you should give them the opportunity to refer you. We often think it doesn't seem right to put more on a person's plate, or we assume they're too busy and don't want to add to anyone's stress. It sounds kind of silly, but that's what many customer service reps think. It's not because of anything negative, but employees just don't want to put more on people's plates. But the truth is, by not asking, you're missing out on some guaranteed referrals. People *want* to refer businesses they love. They really do, and I am going to prove it.

Think about the last great movie or TV show or song that you absolutely loved. What did you do? Did you tell somebody about it? Of course you did! There is something in the brain that compels people to share their pleasurable experiences. It is just built in to the human experience, and if you recommended that movie, show, or song to somebody else, and they loved it in turn, they will tell you so. They'll say, "I can't believe what a great movie you recommended! Thank you! That was awesome!" Then they will tell their friends. This is the how the most successful entertainment projects reach No. 1 status. You hear a song, you love it, and you share it with somebody else, and then they do the same. It's the same for businesses. People want to talk about their experiences with a product or customer service. Don't deprive somebody of the opportunity to share. Make it easy for them to share their experience with family, friends, and co-workers.

That sharing will trickle down to you. When your company grows and the revenues come in, opportunity goes up. If you are a customer service representative, it creates more opportunity

for you. Perhaps it's earning more in commission or being promoted to supervisor or manager. It is all interconnected.

Here are some exercises. Try practicing this dialog:

"I am checking in to see how everything is working with the
product and service."

"I am following up to make sure that the remedy worked
out for you. We appreciate you and your business, and I want to
make sure we talk excellent care of you."

In my business as a customer service training coach, I will
often ask my clients, "How's everything coming along in your
customer training?"

After you lead with these openers, end the call or transaction by asking your customer politely and confidently, "Who
else do you know right now who would benefit from for our
business, product, or service? How about a friend or family
member or a colleague? I promise to contact them and take
excellent care of them."

Practice doing all of these and feel free to customize them
to your taste, then get them in your blood and in your system.

---

45% of U.S. customers will abandon a
transaction if their questions or concerns
are not addressed quickly.

---

In this section, we are going to talk about the three F's of
innovation in customer service: faster, friendlier and fantastic. I love this quote: "Excellent firms don't believe in excel-
lence—only in constant improvement and constant change."

That's from consultant Tom Peters. However, you got to where you are today, whatever made you successful, it could all change tomorrow. I'll give you a perfect example. There was this little multibillion-dollar company a few years back called Blockbuster. Does anybody remember this company? You'd go in there to rent videos on Friday night. You could buy popcorn and candy there—they even sold music CDs. It was a huge company. Blockbuster had an opportunity to buy a little company—you may have heard of it—called Netflix. Blockbuster declined, saying people aren't going to want to have DVDs delivered to their homes. Blockbuster decided to turn away from innovation that would go on to change the entertainment industry. Where is Blockbuster today? They are gone. Where is Netflix today? High in the sky, a multibillion-dollar company!

You have to innovate. You have to look ahead. I mentioned earlier in the book that I used to love to race my motorcycle. Among the lessons I learned from motorcycle racing, the most important is that you have to look ahead because you are going to go where ever you are looking. If I am looking at a wall, that's where I'll end up—heading straight for that wall. If I am looking out at the dirt somewhere, my bike is going to head into the dirt. At 150 miles an hour, whatever happens in that moment will happen in an instant, so it's imperative that the rider knows where they're going and keeps their eyes in that direction. I love that because it's the same with business and the same with customer service. To enhance a customer experience, you, your leaders, and your team of customer service representatives should all be looking in the same direction.

When you have that synergy, when everybody is on the same wavelength and everyone's working toward the same core values and same mission statement, they come up with ways to innovate. To enhance your customer experience, innovation must start at the team level.

*1. How can my company make our service **faster**?*

My daughter is a year old. She keeps climbing out of her crib. Maybe she is going to be a gymnast one day, which is why she keeps crawling out. So, we asked our pediatrician about it, and he suggested trying something called the sleep sack. It's like a little sleeping bag for a baby with little straps. Her arms can move around, but her legs will be wrapped up like a sleeping bag so she can't use them to climb out of the crib. The doctor says this seems to work for a lot of parents in this situation with their children. We went home that after afternoon, and I logged on to my favorite e-commerce site. I type in "sleep sack" and find a ton of brands that make them. I pick out the one I want and enter in my daughter's size, pay for it, and then I get an email that says it's going to be delivered that day. I look at my watch; it was already 2:15 in the afternoon. I'm thinking there is no way this thing is going to get here today. That's impossible. I think it must be a mistake, and I go on with my day. A few hours later there is a knock on the door, and it's the delivery guy dropping off the sleep sack. I was stunned. My baby girl was sleeping in the sleep sack that very night. Unfortunately, the sleep sack didn't work; my daughter still managed to climb out of her crib—but the company still impressed me by getting me the item faster than anything I'd ever experienced from an online transaction. The point of this story is that your competitors are raising the bar through innovation, which means you have to find ways to raise the bar, too.

*2. How can we be **friendlier**?*

There are so many companies now that are super friendly. Companies are also getting better and better at customer service because products and services are getting very similar in quality and pricing. So, when you start looking toward the future, you are going to have to find new ways to compete with other businesses. Successful companies will start competing by besting each other in how well they provide customer service. That's where we're headed. We'll talk a little more about what this looks like in a bit.

*3. How can we make a service more **fantastic**?*

I always tell my clients that they will never be able to stop innovating. The process is ongoing, it's cyclical, it keeps happening. You've got to have A-players on your team who are constantly asking themselves how they can get better. You want employees committed to the mission. You want customers to come away from the experience with your company saying, "Wow! That service was unbelievable! It was fantastic!" You want whatever you do to make them feel cared for.

> **86% of consumers are willing to pay more for an upgraded experience.**

Let's recap this section. There are three ways to enhance your customers' experiences, and innovation is the key to all of them. Ask yourself: How can we make a service faster? How can we make a service friendlier? And how can we make our service more fantastic? If your company embraces innovation, it will continue to grow, and you will continue to get better and better and better. Do it consistently.

> By 2020, a customer will manage 85% of his or her relationship with an enterprise without interacting with a human.
> 89% of businesses are soon expected to compete mainly on customer experience.

The future of customer service is already upon us, and in this section we are going to talk in depth about what that means. Remember the customer service timeline from the 1950s, 1990s, mid-2000s, and 2020 that we discussed in a previous chapter? By the year 2020, it is estimated that 85 percent of a company's customer transactions will not involve any interaction with a live person. This, of course, will depend on your company and your industry, but stop to grasp that fact for a minute: 85 percent of customer transactions will not involve a human being. That's staggering. Also by 2020, experts predict that 89 percent of companies will be competing for customers based not around their product or services but *on their customer service*. That last statistic opens up a real opportunity for you today. When you put together your core values and your mission, you can build a strong foundation to continue to deliver excellent customer service for your company.

It doesn't matter how you deliver it—whether it's over the phone or in person or via social media. You can now have control of what the goal is and how you are going to treat your customers, while the other 85 percent never get to talk to anyone. Whether it is the innovation you design for online customers or the empowerment you give your customer service representatives to meet customer needs—these tools will have a huge impact on your bottom line. When your customer service representatives are empowered to make decisions about what's happening during a transaction, it will clearly show that humans can do this kind of work better than computers and automated systems. When your representative is on the phone, for example, and they hear a baby in the background, they can say, "Do you want me to call you at a later time? You seem busy right now." A human can do that; a computer cannot. That is how you distinguish your business.

> **67% of customers have hung up the phone out of frustration because they could not talk to a real person.**

You have an opportunity to add value to your marketplace, your company, and your customers. Computers and robots are getting smarter and smarter every day. They can do more, and they are getting more responsive than ever before. But as of today, humans still have the winning set of skills that can add value to your customer service and leave the computers and robots in the dust. Only humans can provide your customers with empathy, kindness, and caring to create raving fans. Only you can pick up on verbal and nonverbal cues. Only you can create a custom-made remedy during an interaction with a customer. Only you can build a true relationship with your customers so that they never want to leave you. It's going to be more important than ever as we move into the future. Think about how you can implement all these things into the future.

We are near the end of Chapter 8. Wow! What a journey it has been. You have learned all eight secrets to providing excellent world-class customer service for your clients. But before I conclude my book, let's recap Chapter 8, which focused on solutions.

The first things to remember are that you have to deliver, you have to anticipate, and you have to follow up. You can follow up at your company's location or via email, phone, U.S. mail, text message or other cell phone technology, and through social media platforms. You can also implement a system of customer care calls. Implementing these calls now will double the number of referrals you get within the next 30 days. After a successful transaction, grab the opportunity to ask your customers, "Who else do you know right now who would benefit from your business, product, or service? How about a friend or family member or colleague? I promise to contact them and take excellent care of them." Next, keep striving for greatness by using the three Fs to foster innovation in your company: How can you make your customer service faster, friendlier, and more fantastic? As we move into the future it is going to be more important than ever to stand out. What will matter then is how well you show empathy, kindness, and caring.

Here are some exercises you can try. For the next seven days, try doing a self-assessment after each customer interaction using the questions below. If you really want to get good at this, you can take longer than seven days—but seven is the bare minimum for you to see how implementing the eight secrets all together will work for you. You can take all the things that you have learned in this book and actually get results starting today.

On a scale of 1 to 10 how would you rate your last customer interaction? (If you gave yourself a good rating, try repeating whatever made it good.)

If the interaction was not good, what would you do differently to make it a 10? Write it down in a journal.

Ask yourself: Can you go back to that client and make that interaction a 10? This is a powerful question. If you'd only rate a transaction as a 5 or less—clearly, something went wrong. Can you go back to the client right now and make it better? The client would love it, and that's how you really turn a client around. That client may not have noticed a problem with your interaction, but if you noticed it, then the act of going back and making another effort—another phone call or another email—and offering that customer item of value would make them think you are a rockstar because you made them feel like a rockstar.

What would you do differently with your future customers? You now are armed with a plethora of skills and best practices to choose from that you could adapt for yourself and your industry. After reading this book, you will know what works for you and your customers. You'll begin to use these tools over and over again to great success. Your confidence will go up, and your quality will go up, and your service will go up—and that's how you reach that world-class level.

Don't rest on your laurels, though. When you finally reach that world-class level, the work is only just beginning. You must continue to innovate and get even better.

# CALL TO ACTION

We have reached the end of the book. Thank you for taking this journey with me, and I hope I helped you hone your customer service skills to the best they can be.

Let's stay in touch! Visit me at PureCustomerService.com and enroll in The Pure Customer Service Training Program Online to continue to train your team and implement the strategies in this book. It's an e-learning platform with videos and MP3's to take with you in your car, a workbook, answer key and online assessments. You even get a certificate of completion when your staff finishes the training. Your staff and your company will be PCS certified. You'll get a site badge and certificates that you can share with your customers to show them that you will take excellent care of them. Use the PCS Certified logo in your marketing to attract more customers. Get started today!

Becoming PCS certified tells your prospective clients and customers that you will deliver a world-class experience and that they are your No.1 priority. There are lots of benefits to being certified and here are the top three:

1. PSC certification will provide you with a link you can put on your site with a logo. Anyone who clicks on it will know immediately what it means. But what are the benefits of that? It offers clients peace of mind and offers you a marketing strategy that further distinguishes your organization from your competitors.

2. You can now charge more for your product or service. Remember, if you are associated with brands that are known for their customer service, you can charge more for those services. As we discussed in this book, nine out of 10 customers will pay more for excellent customer service.

3. Your staff will have all it needs to deliver world-class customer service while learning even more about how important great customer service is to your organization.

Do you want to get extraordinary results even faster, easier, and with better results? If so, I am gifting my you a 60-minute customer service strategy call. You will get to talk to a professional, customer service coach and assess your current situation and get customized solutions that you can implement today. It is $500 value, and it's yours for free for buying my book. This is an extra added value that I am giving you to say thank you for being a part of The Pure Customer Service Family. What could happen to your business if you had a professional dive into the challenges specific to your industry or company? This program is not about me, it is about you. So be sure to take advantage of this opportunity. I'm looking forward to serving you. If you have any questions, please give my company, Pure Customer Service, a call at (800) 299-3449, and I promise my staff will take excellent care of you. We would love to see you successful in your customer service journey and taking your customer service to the next level.

Would you like me to come train you or your team live and in person? Or deliver the keynote at your next event? Give us a call or email us today and we promise to take great care of you. I am looking forward to meeting you and your team in person. Call us today at (800) 299-3449.

If you want more free customer service strategies, trainings and best practices, sign up for free at www.PureCustomer Service.com. I'll send you videos, articles, interviews and more. We are glad to have you as a part of our family.

I wish you the highest levels of fulfillment, health and happiness for you and those you care for. Thank you for the opportunity to be your customer service coach. See you soon!

*David Brownlee*

P.S. - Go to www.RockstarCustomerService.com to download customer service calling scripts, content diagrams and cheat sheets that are supplements to this book.

# ABOUT THE AUTHOR

D avid Brownlee is the founder and CEO of The Pure Customer Service Training Company and The Pure Customer Service Certification Program. He is one of the most-watched customer service trainers in history. He has trained over a million businesses and individuals from around the world through his online training, live events, and coaching programs.

He has conducted more than 3,500 one-on-one coaching sessions and has created a training system to take you from where you are now in your customer service to where you want to be.

For the last 20 years, David has been an entrepreneur obsessed with providing his clients with world-class customer service in various industries. He has spent thousands of hours researching best practices and documenting what works in the companies that are delivering amazing customer experiences.

David trains from small businesses to Fortune 500 companies. Some of his past clients include LinkedIn, Harley-Davidson and Behr Paint.

When David is not on the road speaking to companies, he is enjoying his time with his wife, Luna, and his two children in San Diego, California.

CPSIA information can be obtained
at www.ICGtesting.com
Printed in the USA
JSHW032354050922
30154JS00004B/480